ALCHEMISTS, MEDIUMS, AND MAGICIANS

ALSO BY THOMAS CLEARY

ALCHEMISTS, MEDIUMS, AND MAGICIANS

Stories of Taoist Mystics

TRANSLATED AND EDITED BY
THOMAS CLEARY

SHAMBHALA
Boston & London
2009

SHAMBHALA PUBLICATIONS, INC.
Horticultural Hall
300 Massachusetts Avenue
Boston, Massachusetts 02115
www.shambhala.com

9 8 7 6 5 4 3 2 1

First Edition
Printed in Canada

♾ This edition is printed on acid-free paper that meets the American
National Standards Institute z39.48 Standard.
♻ This book was printed on 100% percent postconsumer recycled paper.
For more information please visit us at www.shambhala.com.

Distributed in the United States by Random House, Inc.,
and in Canada by Random House of Canada Ltd

Library of Congress Cataloging-in-Publication Data

Alchemists, mediums, and magicians: stories of Taoist mystics /
translated and edited by Thomas Cleary.
p. cm.
Includes bibliographical references.
ISBN 978-1-59030-659-8 (pbk.: alk. paper)
1. Taoists—China.   2. Taoism—China—History.
I. Cleary, Thomas F., 1949–   II. Title: Stories of Taoist mystics.

BL1910.A53 2009
299.5'14092251—dc22
[B]
2008032446

CONTENTS

TRANSLATOR'S INTRODUCTION

One of the most persistent themes in esoteric thought all over the world is the idea of a secret society surreptitiously superintending human affairs. Such a role has been suggested or suspected of various organizations, both real and imagined, throughout history. The Nine Unknowns of India, the Builders of Egypt, and the Druids of Europe have all been portrayed in this way at various times, as have later groups such as the Masons, Rosicrucians, and Illuminati. Where secular leadership assumed a cultic character, moreover, suspicions of occult connections also came to constitute a commonplace concern in the context of political, military, and economic interests.

Secret societies have played a powerful role in Chinese history, even to the point of organizing open revolt and assuming local functions of secular government. As elsewhere in the world, emperors and kings of all eras in China sought the support of such groups and the counsel and instruction of their masters and adepts. Some associations, to be sure, if not imaginary, have been so secret that their existence outside folklore is scarcely suspected, yet sources of special teaching over the ages, however obscure their actual origins, have undeniably produced many elevated minds and extraordinary personalities that diffused evolutionary ideas of advanced human capacities.

Alchemists, Mediums, and Magicians is a collection of sketches from Chinese history portraying more than one hundred of the remarkable individuals associated with exceptional knowledge, uncommon artistry, and spiritual leadership over a period of more than two millennia. Compiled under the title *Mystic History* by Zhang Tianyu, a Taoist priest in the fourteenth century, this collection introduces a broad range of personalities, professions, and pastimes of China's esoteric elite, from the most illustrious to the utterly obscure. Among them are people who appear to the world as philosophers and scholars, strategists and statesmen, recluses and courtiers, magicians and mediums, philanthropists and educators, alchemists and physicians, seers and soothsayers, priests and paupers, artists and poets.

Alchemists, Mediums, and Magicians introduces an expansive view of the many faces of Taoism and its intimate connection with the core composition of Chinese culture and society. Particular attention is paid to the masters of the Taoist grotto governments that controlled entry into the cave systems where supernal powers were invoked and dangerous mystical exercises were carried out employing powerful consciousness-altering techniques, including sensory deprivation, incantation, visualization, and concentration.

. These secret societies also projected themselves as representative organs of an esoteric government of ascended adepts commanded by an occult hierarchy of immortals, portrayed as realized people of the past who had disappeared but not died. A parallel political practice of imperial beatification, sanctification, and posthumous court appointment of such figures typically included formal appeals to them for divine intercession and assistance from on high.

Alchemists, Mediums, and Magicians features stories from the eleventh century B.C.E. to the thirteenth century C.E., following the course of orthodox dynastic history. Seeking to renew a unifying link between the esoteric and exoteric dimensions of traditional Chinese culture, in his introduction Zhang Tianyu invokes the father of Chinese historiography for a working definition of Taoism to outline the design of this collection:

> The Grand Historian[1] wrote, "Taoism has people's vital spirit unified, acting appropriately without formality, sufficing all people. As for the practical methods, based on the universal order of yin and yang, taking what is good in Confucianism and Moism, distilling the essences of logic and law, they move with the times, change in response to the concrete, establish customs and carry on business in any way appropriate. The instructions are simple and easy to practice; little is done, but with much effect."
>
> I have been inspired to reflect that there must have been such people, but their obscurity has prevented the assertion of the Grand Historian to gain credence in later ages. So I determined

---

1. Sima Qian (ca. 145–90 B.C.E.), called the Grand Historian, was one of the most influential scholars of all time.

to search for them among the people of old. From Lao-tzu on down, I've drawn on their literature on the Way and on virtue and arranged them by categories, as it seems that I've found such people.

In ancient times, when Chuang-tzu set forth the arts of the Way all over the land, he honored Confucius but did not conform; now, emulating his intent, here I make an anthology on Lao-tzu without conformity, as the epitome of honor.

Yang Ziyun[2] said, "Confucius was someone full of culture; Lao-tzu was someone full of mysticism." Accordingly, I have entitled this *Mystic History*. In reality, the origins of Taoism, the extensive and impressive precedents of realized people, are exemplary models for causing the world to flourish and for establishing education.[3] The Grand Historian's proposed definition is what I hope to emulate.

---

2. Yang Ziyun was Yang Xiong, a famous scholar of the Han dynasty.
3. This statement encapsulates the key concern of this collection. It is addressed to the dichotomization of esoteric and exoteric studies and means to say, in essence, that mysticism is not really antisocial, as it is often imagined to be.

ALCHEMISTS, MEDIUMS, AND MAGICIANS

[1]

ZHOU DYNASTY
(traditionally, 1122–221 B.C.E.)

Taoist Virtue and Character[1]

OFFICER XI

Officer Xi was a grandee of Zhou. Adept at inner studies, he regularly consumed vital essences and practiced secret charity. None of the people of his time knew him.

When Lao-tzu traveled west,[2] Xi perceived his atmosphere in advance and knew a real human was going to pass through. Looking to stop him, he actually found Lao-tzu. Lao-tzu knew he was exceptional too, and wrote two works for him, on the Way and on virtue. Afterward he went into the Gobi Desert with Lao-tzu and ate black sesame seed. No one knows where he ended up.

Xi also wrote a book, in nine chapters, called *Keeper of the Pass*.[3] Liu Xiang[4] called it murky and inconsistent, vast and very free, yet with models to make people cool and light, not making people crazy. Chuang-tzu also cites Xi's saying, "It is in oneself without abiding, reveals itself in forming things; like water in movement, like a mirror in stillness, like an echo in response, so indistinct it is as if not

1. This rubric could conceivably be read "Tao-Te Types," invoking association with the school of Lao-tzu as represented by the classic *Tao Te Ching*.
2. Lao-tzu is said to have gone west to escape the disturbed conditions in China as the Zhou dynasty progressively lost its cohesion in the middle of the first millennium B.C.E. It is customarily said that Lao-tzu's destination west was India, but the origin of this theme more likely refers to central Asia, which was linked to China by the Jade Route centuries before the Silk Road. The Kunlun Mountains, an important source of jade, are designated one of the ten regions of immortals in Taoist lore.
3. Cf. *Daozang Jiyao*, vol. 10, pp. 4189–4239.
4. Liu Xiang (79–8 B.C.E.) was a distinguished scholar of the Han dynasty, particularly famous in Taoism for his compilation of legends of immortals.

there, so still it seems clear. Those who assimilate to it harmonize, those who attain it lead; it never precedes people but always follows people."

Xi is famed as one of the great real people of old. He was originally called Master Wenshi, Beginner of Culture.

OFFICER GUI

Officer Gui was styled Gongdu. He was a man of Taiyuan[5] and a cousin of Master Wenshi. He studied widely in the Five Classics.[6] He was particularly learned in astrology, and he transmitted a Taoist book of more than a hundred chapters. He regularly ingested polygonatum tonic.[7]

Before Wenshi met Lao-tzu at Box Canyon Pass, in the times of King Kang and King Zhao of Zhou [1090–1002 B.C.E.],[8] he was living in a reed

---

5. In Shanxi province.

6. The Five Classics, sometimes referred to as the Chinese classics or Confucian classics, normally refers to the *Book of Change* (*I Ching*); the *Classic of Poetry*; the *Ancient Documents*, often referred to as the *Classic of History*; the *Classic of Manners*, also rendered as *Classic of Rites*; and the *Spring and Autumn Annals*. This last work would ostensibly present an anachronism if Officer Gui lived in the early Zhou dynasty, as this account claims, but anachronism is seldom a problem in Taoist legends of immortals. According to Confucian tradition, there was also an ancient *Classic of Music*, which was lost and never recovered.

7. *Polygonatum* is called jade bamboo in Chinese. The rhizome is used in Chinese medicine as a cardiotonic and to relieve certain secondary symptoms of diabetes and pulmonary disease.

8. Conventional history has Lao-tzu an older contemporary of Confucius; the claim that Wenshi was alive hundreds of years earlier in the time of King Zhao (r. 1052–1002 B.C.E.) may be a trace of rivalry with Buddhism. According to the *Annals of White Horse Temple*, omens appeared in China during King Zhao's reign that were interpreted to indicate the birth of a sage in the West whose teaching would spread in China a thousand years later. While modern scholars consider Buddha to have lived in the middle of the first millennium B.C.E., a contemporary of Confucius, Chinese and Tibetan Buddhist traditions place the birth of Buddha five hundred years earlier. The reference to Wenshi as building a lodge dedicated to Taoist practice, suggesting a sort of pseudomonasticism, also seems to suggest an assertion that such an institution was native to China, neither predated nor introduced by Buddhism. Buddhist and Taoist literature both contain all sorts of anachronisms, but for the purposes of mystics these are obscured by the assertion, in the case of Buddhism, that Gautama Buddha was not the first buddha in history, and in the case of Taoism, by the association of Taoist tradition with sages of high antiquity.

hut he had made on Mount Zhongnan;[9] during the reign of King Mu (1001–946 B.C.E.) he rebuilt his reed hut and made it into a temple where he could lodge people who were imbued with the Way. Gongdu subsequently cultivated his practice there with the recluse Du Zhong;[10] he attained the Way and became the Real Human of Great Harmony.

DU ZHONG

Du Zhong was styled Xuanyi. He was a man of Gaojing.[11] When he heard that Wenshi had ascended to truth in 1024 B.C.E.,[12] he went into seclusion in his spiritual abode and studied the Way. At that time five hermits and recluses came from far away.[13] They all sank into silence, empty and aloof, correct and elegant, lofty and plain. Oblivious of all but the arts of the Way, together they projected an impeccable example. This is why King Mu built a temple and shrine for them, installing Du Zhong as the resident Taoist.[14] When he was more than 120 years old he attained the Way and ascended.[15] He is entitled the Real Human of the Absolute.

XIN QIAN

Xin Qian, also called Jiran, was a man from the Pu River region of Mallow Hill.[16] His teacher was Lao-tzu. He studied widely and comprehended everything.

---

9. Distinguished in early Chinese literature, Zhongnan was to become a famous resort for Taoists.

10. Du Zhong is also featured in this collection.

11. Gaojing, in Shaanxi province, was the ancient capital of the Zhou dynasty.

12. In this genre of Taoist literature, ascent to truth normally means death, though it might be called death without prejudice, as it does not bar the reappearance of ascended immortals even centuries later.

13. This story may also have been influenced by the legend of Buddha, according to which his first disciples were five ascetics with whom he had formerly practiced austerities.

14. Carrying the legend of the establishment of the lodge of Wenshi a step further, this image of early institutionalization of Taoism under royal auspices also seems to suggest an assertion of indigenous origin of monasticism, in this sense placing organized Taoism on a par with Buddhism.

15. Here again, to attain the Way and ascend conventionally means to pass away. This usage has some parallel with the practice of referring to the death of a buddha as *parinirvana*, or "absolute nirvana," to distinguish it from the living liberation of nirvana.

16. In Shandong province.

King Ping of Chu[17] asked him, "I hear you attained the Way from Lao-tzu; may I hear it?"

He replied, "The potency of the Way rectifies the crooked and brings order to chaos; for pure virtue to regenerate and the world to be at peace is essentially up to one person. So if you develop virtue you become king, while if you accumulate enmity you get annihilated. This is why Yao and Shun flourished; this is why Jie and Zhou perished."[18]

The king said, "I respectfully hear your directions."

Later he traveled south to Wu and Yue, and Fan Li[19] took him as his teacher. When Yue was going to attack Wu, Li admonished, "I have heard from my teacher that weapons are instruments of ill omen and war is perversity. Conflict is pettiness. Secret plotting, perversity, inclination to use instruments of ill omen, risking life out of pettiness—this will never do." But Gou Jian[20] didn't listen and was defeated at Fushu.

Later Jiran was appointed to the rank of superior grandee, but he didn't accept it, instead going into seclusion in the mountains. He wrote a book in twelve scrolls, calling himself Wen-tzu.[21] The language and doctrine are both based on Lao-tzu. Liu Zihou[22] edited it to bring out the meaning more. One section says, "Spirit is the font of intelligence; when spirit is pure, intelligence is clear. Intelligence is the capital of mind; when intelligence is impartial, the mind is even." It also says, "Higher learning is heard by spirit, middle learning is heard by mind, lower learning is heard by ear." It also says, "When people are highly ranked, watch what they recommend; when they are wealthy, watch what they want; when they are poor,

---

17. R. 528–516 B.C.E.

18. Yao and Shun were nonhereditary predynastic kings of the third millennium B.C.E. conventionally cited as models of virtue. Jie (r. 1818–1766 B.C.E.), last king of the Xia dynasty, and Zhou (r. 1154–1122 B.C.E.), last king of the Shang dynasty, are conventionally cited as paragons of self-indulgence and vice.

19. See the story of Fan Li.

20. Gou Jian was king of Yue from 496 to 465 B.C.E. Though Yue eventually annexed Wu, at one point Gou was defeated in battle and taken prisoner.

21. For an English translation of the received version, see *Wen-tzu* by Thomas Cleary (1992).

22. A famous scholar and poet of the Tang dynasty, who lived from 773 to 819.

watch what they'll accept." It also says, "Human nature wants peace, but indulgence in desires spoils this." This is but a sliver of *Wen-tzu*.

In the Tianbao era (742–755) Wen-tzu was entitled Real Human Penetrating the Mysteries, and his book was called *Understanding the Mysteries: A Scripture on Reality*.

LU TONG

Lu Tong was the madman of Chu called the Carriage Grabber. He liked nurturing life and would gather and eat radishes, fruits, and turnips. He traveled around to famous mountains, and people saw him for several hundred years.

When Confucius was going to Chu, the Carriage Grabber passed Confucius, saying, "Oh phoenix, oh phoenix, how virtue has declined! Those who are gone cannot be admonished, those yet to come can still be pursued. Stop, stop! Those who participate in government now are in peril."

Confucius alighted, wanting to talk with him, but he ran away, so Confucius didn't get to talk to him.[23]

GENGSANG CHU

Gengsang Chu, a man of Chen, was an employee of Lao-tzu and had the best understanding of his Way. He lived in the Weilei Mountains.[24] He dismissed servants who were obviously bright and kept away from maids who were attentively kind, staying with the intractable and employing the unkempt.

After he had lived there for three years, the Weilei Mountains became very fertile and rich. Later he traveled to Wu and lived in seclusion on Bowl Peak in Piling.[25] That is the location of the ancient Temple of the Open Spirit. He wrote a book in nine chapters called *Master Gengsang*, also called *The Master of the Hidden Storehouse*.[26]

23. Cf. *Lunyu* 18.5.
24. Said to be in Lu, in Shandong; also said to be in Liang province, which in Zhou times would refer to one of the nine provinces of antiquity, including southern Shaanxi and part of Sichuan.
25. In Jiangsu.
26. For an English translation, see *Thunder in the Sky* by Thomas Cleary (1993).

The book was lost, but during the Kaiyuan era (713–741) of the Tang dynasty, Wang Bao presented that book to the throne. Because of that, Gengsang was entitled the Real Human of Open Spirituality, and his book was entitled *Open Spirituality: A Scripture on Reality.*

NANRONG CHU

Nanrong Chu met Lao-tzu. Lao-tzu said, "Why did you come with such a crowd?" Alarmed, Chu looked behind him. Lao-tzu said, "You don't know what I mean?" Chu looked down, embarrassed. Then he looked up and said with a sigh, "Now I have forgotten my answer, so I've lost my question."

Lao-tzu said, "What do you mean?"

He said, "If I don't know, people will say I'm ignorant. If I do know, instead I'll be anxious for myself. To be inhumane hurts people, but to be humane means one worries about oneself instead. Injustice injures others, but to be just means one worries about oneself instead. How can I escape this?"

Lao-tzu said, "Can you embrace unity? Can you avoid losing it? Can you leave others alone and look for it in yourself? Can you be prompt, can you be simple? Can you be childlike? A small child moves without cognizing its doings, goes without knowing where, its body like a branch of a withered tree, its mind like dead ashes. If one is like this, fortune does not come, but neither does calamity. If there is no fortune or calamity, how can there be human trouble?"

At first Chu took Master Gengsang as his teacher. That master said, "I have little ability, not enough to teach you. Why don't you go south to see Lao-tzu?" So Chu saw Lao-tzu and requested permission to ask him questions on account of Master Gengsang.

OFFICER WEN

Master Yinwen studied the Way with Lao-tzu. He made a Flower Mountain hat[27] to express it himself. In his practice of the Way he

27. A Flower Mountain (Huashan) hat is described as even above and below, symbolizing equality. Huashan is a central reference point in the domain of Taoist topography.

didn't bother with social conventions or put on appearances for people. He wished for the world to be at peace, to let the people live, with a sufficiency of nutrition for everyone, that's all. Unashamed to be treated with contempt, he resolved people's disputes for them. Forbidding aggression, laying down arms, he saved society from war. One who didn't forget the world, he went all over the land this way, lecturing the rulers and educating the subjects. His book, in two chapters, is called *Master Yinwen.*[28]

DUCHENG QI

Ducheng Qi was a reclusive gentleman of Zhou. He made a long journey to see Lao-tzu. He said, "I've heard you're a sage, so I didn't mind coming from afar; I'd like to ask about self-cultivation."

Lao-tzu said, "The Way does not end with the great, is not lost in the small. It is so vast there is nothing it does not contain, so deep it cannot be fathomed. Fully developed people find out the reality of things and are able to keep to the fundamental. Therefore they are beyond heaven and earth, detached from myriad things, so their spirits are never wearied."

Ducheng Qi had some attainment of this.

CUI JU

Cui Ju was a wise grandee of Zhou. He asked Lao-tzu, "How is it possible to improve the human mind without governing the world?"

Lao-tzu said, "You should be careful not to attract the human mind. The human mind presses down and pushes up, so above and below imprison and kill. It is hotter than fire, colder than ice, swifter than a glance, and circles beyond the four seas. It is profoundly still in repose, far-reaching and forward in action. Restless, arrogant, and unbridled—that's the human mind!

---

28. In the Qing dynasty collection *Siku tiyao,* this book is categorized in the *zi* (philosopher/master) section as *zajialei* (syncretists). The *Huainanzi,* a Han dynasty Taoist classic, has also been put in the syncretist category by scholastics.

"In ancient times, the Yellow Emperor[29] first attracted people's hearts by humanity and justice. Handed over to the Three Kings,[30] the world got very upset. At this stage, the happy and the irate suspected each other, the ignorant and the educated cheated each other, the

29. The Yellow Emperor is supposed to have reigned for a hundred years, from 2698 to 2598 B.C.E. He is one of the most important culture heroes of Chinese and Taoist legend. According to the Taoist classic *Lieh-tzu*, for fifteen years after assuming the throne, the Yellow Emperor was delighted that everyone supported him; he nourished his natural life and enjoyed the pleasures of the senses. In the process he became gaunt and dark, confused and emotionally disturbed.

Then for another fifteen years he worried about disorder in the land; using all of his intelligence and mental energy, he managed the hundred clans. In the process, he became gaunt and dark, confused and emotionally disturbed.

Finally the Yellow Emperor lamented, "My fault has been excess. Such is the trouble involved in taking care of oneself; such is the trouble of governing everything."

At this point he set aside his administrative activities, stopped sleeping in his seraglio, sent away his servants, suspended musical performances, cut down on cuisine, and retired into solitude to purify his mind and get control over his body, taking no personal role in government for three months.

Taking a nap one day, he dreamed he traveled to Shangri-la, west of the province of Yan, north of the province of Tai, untold thousands of miles from the country of Qi; it could not be reached by boat, carriage, or foot but only by spiritual travel. In that country there were no political leaders, just a state of nature. The people had no habits or cravings, they were just natural. They didn't know to like life or to detest death, so there was no premature death. They didn't know to prefer themselves to others, so there was no love or hatred. They didn't know how to rebel or obey, so there was no profit or harm. They had no attachments, so they had no fears. They didn't drown in water, didn't burn in fire. They were not hurt by hitting, were not pained by scratching. They rode the air like walking on the ground, slept in space as if in bed. Clouds and fog did not obstruct their vision, thunder did not distort their hearing, beauty and ugliness did not distort their minds. Mountains and valleys did not trip them up, for they traveled only in spirit.

When the Yellow Emperor woke up, he was happy and content. Summoning his three deputies, he said to them, "I lived alone for three months, purifying my mind and mastering my body, contemplating a way to live and to govern, but I failed to grasp the art. Tired, I took a nap, and this is what I dreamed. Now I know that the supreme Tao cannot be sought subjectively. Now I realize this; now I have grasped this, yet I cannot tell it to you."

For the next twenty-eight years the whole land was at peace, like that mythical country, until the emperor passed on. The populace mourned him for more than two hundred years.

30. The Three Kings refers to the founders of the Xia, Shang, and Zhou dynasties of preimperial China. A merit-based conception of leadership in China views hereditary rulership as devolutionary.

good and the bad repudiated each other, the false and the truthful reviled each other, and society degenerated. Great virtues disintegrated, and nature and life became dissociated. Everyone was eager for knowledge, and the peasants wanted to have everything. At this stage, axes and saws were used to dismember people, marking cords were used to strangle them, hammer and chisels were used to maim them. The whole world was a mess, and the fault was in attracting the human mind."

Lao-tzu was indignant at the degeneration of morals and took the opportunity of Cui Ju's question to warn the world.

Bo Ju

Bo Ju was a chief minister of Zhou who learned from Lao-tzu. He traveled to Qi, where he saw a man who'd been executed. Doffing his court robe to cover the man, he cried to heaven, mourning him, saying, "Oh, man! The world is experiencing a great disaster; you alone are the first to leave it! It is said, 'Don't steal, don't kill.' Once glory and disgrace are defined, then you see objects of concern; once money and goods accumulate, then you see objects of contention. When people are exhausted physically, not allowed a moment's rest, how could they not come to this?

"Rulers of ancient times attributed successes to the people while blaming failures on themselves; they attributed correctness to the people while attributing error to themselves. So if even one person lost his life, they'd withdraw and blame themselves. Now it is otherwise. They hide things so the ignorant don't know; they create tremendous difficulties, then punish those who lack the daring; they impose tremendous responsibilities, then penalize those who can't cope; they make the road long, then execute those who do not arrive.

"When the people run out of savvy and strength, they use falsehood to go on. With each day producing so many falsehoods, how can the people choose not to contrive falsehood? For when their strength is insufficient, they contrive falsehood; when their knowledge is insufficient, they deceive; when they don't have enough to live on, they steal. When robbery and theft are rampant, who can be blamed?"

Many of Bo Ju's sayings were gotten from Lao-tzu.

LIE YUKOU

Lie Yukou was a man of Zheng, a contemporary of Duke Xu of Zheng.[31] His learning was derived from the Yellow Emperor and Lao-tzu. He lived in the game preserve of Zheng for forty years without anyone's recognizing him.

He first attended the Master of Pot Hill; later he took Old Mr. Shang as his teacher and associated with Elder Ignorant Nobody. After nine years of progress on the Way of the two masters, he was able to ride the wind.

His disciple Yan Hui asked, "Does anyone who asks about the Way strive for wealth?"

Liezi said, "Jie and Zhou just slighted the Way and valued profit; that is why they perished."

When Master Lie was destitute, his face had the look of hunger. A visitor told [Prime minister] Ziyang of Zheng about this and said, "Lie Yukou is a man with the Way; if he lives in your domain yet is destitute, will you not be considered unappreciative of gentlemen?" So Ziyang of Zheng had an officer send Lie Yukou some grain. Master Lie came out and met the courier, bowed twice, and refused the gift. The courier left, and Master Lie went back inside. His wife, watching this, beat her breast and said, "I've heard that the wives and children of those who have the Way all enjoy ease and comfort. Now you're showing signs of starvation and the lord sends you food to eat, but you don't take it. It isn't fate, is it?"

Master Lie laughed and said to her, "The lord doesn't know me himself; he sent me grain on the word of another. Were he to punish me, that too would be on the word of another. That's why I don't accept." As it turned out, in fact the people attacked and killed Ziyang.[32]

---

31. R. 421–395 B.C.E.

32. Ziyang introduced Legalism in the state of Zheng. As a result of the establishment of the rule of law, it is said, Zheng became peaceful under the administration of Ziyang. Commentary on the *Lieh-tzu*, from which this account is taken, says that there were many savants living in the wilds of Zheng at that time. The implication is that these savants had taken refuge there from the widespread turmoil of the era. The rule of law under Legalist principles withdrew certain customary privileges from the old aristocracies, and Ziyang was not the only Legalist in Chinese history to be murdered by influential enemies. Gongsun Yang, the Lord of Shang, who introduced Legalist policies to engineer the rise of the state of Qin to a position of preeminent power during the era of the Warring States, was drawn and quartered, after the king he had worked for passed away, by people who had held a grudge against him for more than twenty-five years.

He spoke like this because he couldn't forget his feelings about this world. Coming to where he says, "The phoenix is the vitality of yang, the unicorn is the vitality of yin, the populace is the vitality of virtue," now this is genius indeed! Jia Yi's[47] *Ode to the Copper Pheasant* is said to take a lot of his words.

47. Jia Yi (200–168 B.C.E.) was a distinguished scholar, author, and statesman of the Han dynasty. He appears in the story of Sima Chu below.

[2]

QIN DYNASTY
(246–206 B.C.E.)

Taoist Character[1]

GUO SICHAO

Guo Sichao was a man from the state of Yan. Of four brothers who all attained the Way, Sichao was the eldest. He lived on Mount Leiping of Huayang;[2] there he planted five kinds of fruit. This soil was also suitable for planting crabapple; as it is said, the crabapples of a wealthy locale are used to ward off the severity of disasters.

In front of the dwelling was a pond that Sichao constructed. Sichao used to sport about in it in a small boat. Tapping the side of the boat, he'd sing,

> The clear pond comes with a miraculous cave;
> The primeval forest is thick with green leeks.
> Dark birds circle the dim fields,
> Conversation comes out in the calm.
> Drumming the oars, riding the mystic waves,
> I bow my head, hoping for a morning breeze.
> Having no assurance of liberation as yet,
> I roam in the hills and forests.

1. The word used here for *character* means an item, type, class, or level of quality; in reference to people it is applied to personal qualities or character. Used alone it always implies goodness, as when it is said that a person has character, what is meant is good character.

2. *Huayang* means south of Mount Hua (Huashan, or Flower Mountain), an important reference point in Taoist topography. For a modern account of a Taoist pilgrimage to Mount Hua, see *Opening the Dragon Gate* by Chen Kaiguo and Zheng Shunchao (1996), chap. 12.

Folding away these miraculous phoenix feathers,
I conceal my flowery dragon scales.
Transcending the world is something in the mind;
Myriad gusts are all dirt and dust.
I look with pity on the cicada hatched in the morning—
Who will complete your cycle?

Roaming in the void, I escape the high winds;
Walking in the miraculous, I have no form or place.
The experience of completeness lights the dawn haze;
Nine phoenixes sing in the morning sun.
Spreading their wings, they dwarf the Milky Way.
Flying around auspicious clouds over the lingering fog,
Ultimately reaching the abode of the Great Subtlety,
I take the gold pear broth,
And roam beyond the mystic borders,
Neither existing nor passing away.

Riding the wind, dancing in the spiritual sky,
Dressed in mist, cinched with nine suns,
Into high space I direct the dragon wheels,
Finally arriving at the North Flower Room.
The spiritual tiger passes through the coral forest,
Wind and clouds combine into one.
Opening the door to the hidden darkness,
The spiritual transformation is mysteriously traceless.

After he attained the Way, he assisted the Immortal Lord of the Left in the Nine Palaces on high and received the title Parasol-Holding Gentleman of the Jade Terrace.

An imperial document of the Xuanhe era of the Song dynasty says, "The hidden miracles of the Three Energies are certainly not to be measured in words; the congealing of myriad spirits does not admit of a hesitating quest. General praise is a prelude to higher reality; the truth opens up to the ultimate Way. The real human Guo, esquire of the Jade Terrace, has reached completion of achievement and is ranked among those of the Nine Palaces. Internalizing the reflection of the moon, he has already flown into infinity. Holding a flower parasol, here he waits entirely on the Emperor of the Void. Since he's opened up the net of the elemental, it is fitting he should be elevated by an illustrious name. We also hope he will qualify to assist forever our aims for prosperity. He is to be especially entitled the Real Human Preserving the Light of the Greatest Subtlety."

JIANG SHUMO

Jiang Shumo was the lord of Baling in Qin times. He went into hiding on Mount Juqu.[3] There he planted five kinds of fruit and five kinds of bitter herbs, which he sold to buy cinnabar for his use. The fact that there are still shallots, leeks, onions, and scallions on that mountain even now may be a result of his plantings.

After he attained immortality, he once wrote a letter to an officer of the infinite, saying, "In the past I studied the Way in Demon Valley, gained the Way on Few Houses Mountain,[4] groomed my wings in Huayang, and awaited takeoff in the realm of escape. Riding in the chariot of the wind at times, I repose on Juqu. Words of warning always lament the rapidity of the passing of generations. Things remain while the people disappear—what's the point of my toiling?"

3. This is the mountain often referred to as Maoshan, or the Maos' Mountain, an erstwhile gold mine eventually to become a principal center of Taoism, the eighth of the Ten Great Grotto Heavens. See the story of the three Mao masters below.
4. Few Houses Mountain is the site of the Shaolin Temple, which was later to become known in Buddhist tradition as the lodge of the Indian monk Bodhidharma, who is said to have founded the Chan sect of Buddhism.

[3]

WESTERN HAN DYNASTY
(206 B.C.E.–8 C.E.)

Tao and Secular Power[1]

ZHANG LIANG

Zhang Liang was styled Zifang. His ancestors were people of the state of Han. When Qin destroyed Han, Liang used his family fortune to hire assassins to kill the king of Qin to avenge Han, as his forbears had been ministers of the state of Han for five generations.

Liang used to study rites in Haiyang. In the East he met the Lord of the Blue Sea,[2] found a strongman, and made an iron mallet weighing 120 pounds. When the king of Qin traveled east, Liang and his assassins launched an attack on him but mistakenly hit an accompanying chariot. The king of Qin was furious and had the offenders sought in a great hurry.

Liang then changed his name and fled into hiding.

Once Liang was strolling along an earthen bridge when an old man dressed in coarse wool came up to him, dropped one of his shoes off the bridge, then looked at him and said, "Mr. Scholar, go down and get my shoe." Liang was taken aback and wanted to drive him away. But he forced himself to be patient and went down and got the shoe, presenting it on his knees. The old man took it on his foot and said, "Mr. Scholar, you can be taught. Meet me here at dawn in five days." Liang thought it strange, but he assented, still on his knees.

Five days later Liang went, but the old man was already there. "Why are you late?" he said angrily.

---

1. The word used for *secular power* here means weighing, balancing, hence used of political authority and also of tactical strategy.
2. This refers to one of the so-called Isles of the Immortals of Taoist legend.

Five days later he went at cock's crow, but again the old man was already there. Again he said angrily, "Why are you late?"

Five days later he went in the middle of the night. After a while the old man also showed up. Pleased, he said, "This is how it should be." Bringing out a book, he said, "If you read this, you'll be a teacher of royalty. After ten years you'll prosper. In thirteen years you'll see me north of Qi; the yellow stone at the foot of Mount Gucheng will be me." Then he left and disappeared.

When morning came, Liang looked at the book; it was *Taigong's Art of War.*[3] Considering it unusual, he used to study it. He became a soldier of fortune and used the book to win over Liu Bang.[4] Liu Bang liked it and always applied its tactics, ultimately using them to take over the empire.

Zhang Liang then went along with the new emperor when he established his capital city. Being sickly by nature, he spent more than a year in seclusion doing energy induction exercises and not eating grain.

When the emperor wanted to get rid of his eldest son, the crown prince, and set up the son of Lady Qi, Empress Lu consulted Zhang Liang for strategy and, based on that, brought four elders from Mount Shangluo to attend the crown prince over wine. After the wine, as it turned out, the emperor didn't replace the crown prince after all; this was the effect of Liang's plan to invite the four elders.

Liang then declared, "My family were ministers to the state of Han for generations. When Han was destroyed, I did not spare a fortune in gold to avenge Han. Now I've become teacher of an emperor merely by talking, with an income from ten thousand households and a rank among the lords. This is the pinnacle for a commoner; it is enough for me. I wish to abandon the concerns of human society and follow the Master of the Red Pines in his wanderings." So he studied the Way, wishing to ascend. When he died, he was given the posthumous title Lord Wencheng.

Thirteen years after Liang first met that old man, he went through the north of Qi in the company of the emperor. He actually saw a yellow stone at the foot of Mount Gucheng; he took it and enshrined it as a treasure. When Liang died, they interred the yellow stone with

3. Taigong was Jiang Shang, adviser to the founders of the Zhou dynasty.
4. Liu Bang was to found the Han dynasty, which succeeded the Qin.

him. At every summer and winter ceremony at the tomb, there was a ritual of gratitude to the yellow stone.

The Temple of Divine Inspiration in Chenliu prefecture is where he is propitiated. In the Zhenghe era of the Song dynasty he was entitled the Space-Traversing Real Human.

Cao Can

Cao Can was a man of Bei. During the Qin dynasty he had been a prison warden while Xiao He was a chief deputy, an important officer in the prefecture where he lived.

When the Exalted Ancestor [founder of the Han dynasty] was the Duke of Bei, Cao Can served as his attendant. In 194 B.C.E., the first year of the reign of Emperor Hui of the Han dynasty, Can was made prime minister of the state of Qi.

When Can administered the state of Qi, Qi had seventy walled cities. When the empire was first pacified, King Zhuohui of Qi was advanced in age. Can summoned all the elders and scholars and asked them how to settle the peasants. Because it was Qi, there were hundreds of Confucians; they all said different things, and Can didn't know what to decide.

Hearing of a Mr. Gai who had mastered the Huang-Lao teachings, Cao Can sent people with generous gifts to invite him. Mr. Gai told him that if government policy values purity and calm, the people will stabilize themselves. He went on in this vein, giving a thorough account of it. Cao Can now vacated his official residence and housed Mr. Gai there.

Cao Can's administration essentially used Huang-Lao techniques, so in the nine years that he governed there the state of Qi was peaceful, and he was highly praised as a wise minister.

On the death of Xiao He, who was prime minister at the time, Cao Can replaced him, changing nothing of his operations, following He's commitment completely. With his magnanimity, generosity, purity, and serenity, he was a model for the whole empire. He was prime minister for three years. When he died, he was given the posthumous title Elegant Lord.

A peasant song says, "When Xiao He made the law, he explained it like drawing a line; when Cao Can succeeded him, he kept it without fail. Thanks to their purity and serenity, the people were peaceful and unified."

Taoist Character

SIMA JIZHU

Sima Jizhu was a man of Chu. He told fortunes at the eastern market of Chang'an.

Song Zhong was a court grandee, and Jia Yi was a professor. They both went out to the baths one day, debating as they went along, citing and discussing the arts of the Way of ancient kings and sages. Surveying the human condition, they looked at each other and sighed in lament.

Jia Yi said, "I've heard that sages of ancient times were not at court but were to be found among diviners and physicians." The two then took a carriage to the city and roamed around among the fortune-tellers' stalls.

It had just rained, and there were few people in the streets. Sima Jizhu was sitting in a leisurely manner, attended by three or four disciples, in the process of analyzing the ways of heaven and earth, the movements of the sun and moon, the roots of fortune and calamity in yin and yang.

The two grandees presented themselves with a bow. Jizhu looked at them and saw that they appeared to have some knowledge, so he was courteous to them and had his students offer them seats.

Once they had sat down, Jizhu resumed his previous talk. Zhong and Yi were awed and enlightened; straightening their scholar collars and sitting up, they said, "We've observed your condition and heard your words. We've never seen your like in all the world; why are you living in such humble circumstances and carrying on such a mean trade?"

Jizhu laughed out loud, holding his belly. "I observed you grandees to seem to have Taoist arts—how come your talk is so low and your words so uncivilized? Now, what do you consider wisdom? Whom do you esteem? Now, why do you demean and besmirch an elder? What you say is nothing but respect for titles and grants, debasing diviners." Jizhu went on and on, speaking hundreds of words, citing Lao-tzu and Chuang-tzu, profoundly illumining the Way and virtue, to say that divining has benefits for people.

Song Zhong and Jia Yi were stunned. They were so taken aback they were speechless. They bowed again and took leave. Going out the gate of the marketplace, they could barely manage to get into their carriage.

Leaning on the bowing board with their heads down, they couldn't muster any energy.

Three days later, Song saw Jia outside the palace gate; pulling him aside to speak privately, he sighed to himself and said, "The loftier the way, the safer one is; the higher the authority, the greater the danger. Living in a glorious condition, one day we'll lose our status. Now, if you err in fortune-telling, you don't get deprived of your life, but if you are in charge of strategy for another and make mistakes, you have no place to rest. The difference is tremendous, like the cap of the sky versus the shoes of the earth. This is what Lao-tzu refers to in saying, 'The nameless is the beginning of myriad things.' Heaven and earth are wide and vast, with multitudes of people, some safe, some in danger, no one knowing where to settle them. For you and me, what's the use of having anything to do with them? The longer they go on, the more complacent they are; even the justice of Master Zeng[5] would make no difference."

Song Zhong was subsequently sent as an ambassador to the Huns, but he came back without have reached there, so he was executed. Jia Yi became tutor to King Huai of Liang; when the king fell from a horse and died, Yi wouldn't eat and died in bitterness. These were examples of people who cut off the root working on the flowers.

According to *Declarations of the Realized*, Jizhu later went into a cave on Mount Weiyu[6] and received from the Woman of the Great Mystery[7] a method of changing the body by the impression of the treasury of golden light in the essence of stone. When he was about to depart, he arranged his pillow and mat into an image to substitute for

5. Zeng Can, one of the greatest disciples of Confucius.

6. In Zhejiang; an important place in Taoist legend and topography.

7. Zhuan He, called Xiling Zidou, a female adept to whom were attributed extraordinary powers, including reviving the dead. After her father died when she was young, she and her mother were told they would also die prematurely. As a consequence, she sought and obtained Taoist arts. One of the powers she is said to have acquired and transmitted to certain disciples, that of projecting multiple appearances, is also attributed to Zhang Daoling, the first of the Celestial Masters. It resembles the power attributed to the Buddhist nun Simhavijurmbhita in the *Avatamsaka Sutra*, an important source for central Asian Buddhists introducing Buddhism into China. One of the early extracts from this immense compilation, the *Pusa benye jing*, translated into Chinese in the third century by a multilingual layman from central Asia, lists "ascended immortals" and "celestial masters" among the examples of different names given to buddhas in various cultures, explicitly connecting Buddhist and Taoist paths.

himself. His tomb is in Shu prefecture, on the south side of Chengdu's Bowl Mountain.

Zhuge Liang, Lord of Warriors,[8] set up a tablet in front of his grave a long time ago, memorializing his virtues: at the end of the paean on the tablet it says, "Mystic infinity, absolutely silent, combines yin and yang. As heaven and earth melt together, myriad species appear in profusion. The master's logic was clear; he distinguished the flexible and the firm. When he observed through the agency of ghosts and spirits, the six measures were manifestly clear."[9]

Also, Jizhu had one son and one daughter, who both attained the Way. His son was named Fayu, his daughter was named Jihua. They all lived on Mount Weiyu.

Jizhu read Jade scriptures,[10] ingested essences of luminous elixir, and absorbed dawn sunlight. At this time his face looked like that of a twenty-year-old maiden, while his beard was three feet long and black as ink. Such is the Way of the Lord Noble of the East—a truly extraordinary thing.

Tao and Government[11]

DONGFANG SHUO

Dongfang Shuo was styled Manqing. He was a man of Yanci in Pingyuan.[12] He lived in Wu for a long time and was a teacher of writing

---

8. Zhuge Liang was a famous military and civil leader. See *Daozang jiyao*, vols. 22–23, pp. 9917 et passim. For his writings on leadership, see *Mastering the Art of War* by Thomas Cleary (1989).

9. The *six measures* refers to the plumb line, level, compass, balance, square, and scale. These are cited collectively to stand for capacities of assessment and evaluation in all domains of experience.

10. This could apply to a number of texts but probably refers to the *Yellow Court* corpus. According to *Legends of Spiritual Immortals of the Wang Clan*, Wang Tan, who would become a disciple of both Xiling Zidou (see n. 7 above) and Sima Jizhu, had previously learned the secrets of inner cultivation according to the *Yellow Court* teaching and is honorifically entitled the Realized Man of the Yellow Court. See *Daozang jiyao*, vol. 6.

11. The word for *government* used here means "influence" and is used to imply the moral and educational elements of leadership.

12. In Shandong.

for decades. In the time of Emperor Wu (140–86 B.C.E.) he submitted a document discussing expedients and was made a court gentleman. By the time of Emperor Zhao (86–74 B.C.E.), some contemporaries called him a sage; others said he was an ordinary man. His behavior was sometimes deep, sometimes shallow, sometimes open, sometimes silent; sometimes he spoke sincerely, sometimes he spoke in jest. No one knew his point.

Then in the beginning of the reign of Emperor Xuan (73–49 B.C.E.), he gave up his position as court gentleman to escape the turmoil of the times. Setting down his turban at his official quarters, he disappeared as the wind blew it away. Later he was seen around Huiji[13] and peddling medicine on the Five Lakes. Those who recognized him suspected he might be the spirit of the plant Jupiter.

Xiahou Zhan[14] wrote a eulogy for his image:

> With initiative and efficiency,
> A clear and open mind,
> And a universal embrace,
> He looked down on prime ministers,
> Laughed in derision at great men.
> His mental capacity was unprecedented;
> He trod upon prestige and power.
> When prominent, he didn't celebrate distinction;
> When lowly, he was not distressed.
> He would joke with a powerful lord
> As with a colleague or friend;
> He looked upon his peers as insignificant.
> Outstanding in integrity, beyond the norm,
> His lofty mentality eclipsing the age,
> He can be said to be one beyond the crowd
> Who roamed outside of convention.

Yang Xiong[15] also portrayed Shuo as broadminded and complex, not known for one practice. He could respond to situations adaptively like an actor; he was never at a loss, seeming knowledgeable; criticiz-

---

13. A mountain complex in Zhejiang.
14. Lived from 243 to 291. A court gentleman of the Jin dynasty.
15. Lived from 53 B.C.E. to 18 C.E.

ing directly, he seemed honest; acting immorally, he seemed insane. If he was not a Bo Yi or a Shu Qi,[16] then he was a Liuxia Hui.[17] He admonished his son on the aforementioned appearances:

> Bo Yi and Shu Qi were clumsy,
> Lao-tzu was clever.
> Eat your fill, walk at ease;
> Serve in government instead of farming.
> Keep hidden and play with the world;
> Turn away from the times, not toward.

He was certainly an outstanding joker!

Yan, the Duke of Lu [705–789] composed a eulogy for his portrait and an inscription for the back of his memorial tablet. Both are in De province.

Taoist Scholarship[18]

SIMA TAN

Sima Tan's forbears were chief astrologers for the Zhou dynasty. As chief astrologer, Tan learned astronomy from Tang Dou, received the *Changes* from Yang He, and studied treatises on the Way with Huangzi. He served in office from 140 to 105 B.C.E. Feeling pity that students didn't understand their ideas and the teachers differed, he discoursed on the essential points of the six schools in these terms:

16. Bo Yi and Shu Qi, icons of classical morality, were brothers who each left their homeland so the other could inherit the patrimony. Later, when their state was annexed by King Wu of the nascent Zhou dynasty, the brothers "refused to eat the grain of Zhou" and disappeared into the mountains, where they starved to death.

17. Liuxia Hui is another icon of Confucian morality. In *Lunyu* 18.2, Confucius says, "When Liuxia Hui was a chief judge, he was dismissed from office three times. People said, 'Shouldn't you leave?' He said, 'If I work for people in an honest way, where can I go and not get dismissed three times? If I worked for people in a crooked way, why would I have to leave my hometown?'"

18. The word used for *scholarship* here conventionally refers to Confucian scholars, but its original meaning is broader, and there is a different expression to specify *Confucian*, if necessary. One of the intentions of this collection was to transcend artificial boundaries between Confucianism and Taoism within the greater unity of Chinese culture.

"The 'Great Tradition' of the *Changes* says, 'The world is ultimately one, yet there are a hundred considerations; the goal is the same, but there are different routes.' The schools of Yin-Yang, Confucianism, Moism, Logic, Legalism, and Taoism are concerned with government; it's just that the different routes they follow in their arguments are more or less concise.

"As I view the Yin-Yang arts, they are very detailed, involving many taboos, making people inhibited and fearful. Nevertheless, their exposition of the overall order of the four seasons cannot be lost.

"Confucians are learned but lacking in focus. They work hard but accomplish little. Therefore their premises are hard to follow completely. Nevertheless, their exposition of the courtesies between ruler and subject and father and son, and their systematization of gender and age distinctions, cannot be challenged.

"Moism is austere and hard to follow, so its practice cannot be pursued exclusively. Nevertheless its fortification of basics and moderation of consumption are indispensable.

"Legalism is strict, with little mercy, but its correctness in distinction of ruler and subject, superior and subordinates, is irreplaceable.

"Logicians make people careful but prone to miss reality. Nevertheless their correction of names and actualities cannot be ignored.

"Taoists don't do anything yet also say there's nothing they don't do. The reality is easy to practice, but the terminology is hard to understand. Their arts are based on empty nothingness, functioning by adaptive accord. They have no established structure, no permanent form; therefore they are able to find out the conditions of all things. They are not leaders or followers of anyone, therefore they can be masters of everyone. Whether they have laws or no laws is a function of the time; whether they have measures or no measures depends on the people for whom measures are to be promoted or abandoned.

"So it is said 'Sages do not become obsolete, for timely change is their discipline. Emptiness is the constant of the Way; adaptation is the mainstay of rulers.' When all ministers are equally adept, their responsibilities are each self-evident.

"When the reality matches the name, this is called correct; when the reality doesn't match the name, this is called vain. When vain words are not given a hearing, criminals don't breed; when the worthy and unworthy are distinct of themselves, good and bad then take shape. It's just a matter of what you need to use; what cannot be accomplished? Then you accord with the Great Way, wholly merged with the infinite mystery; light illumines the world, then returns to the nameless.

"What animates people is spirit, what supports people is the body. If the spirit is overused it gets exhausted, while if the body is over-worked it wears out. When the spirit and the body separate, then you die. The dead cannot be restored to life, what has been separated can-not be rejoined; therefore sages are careful of this.

"From this perspective, the spirit is the basis of life, while the body is the implement of life. If you don't first stabilize your spirit and body yet say you have the means to govern the world, how can that be?"

Tan's son Sima Qian[19] succeeded him and published his sayings.

Taoist Influence

MEI FU

Mei Fu was styled Zizhen. He was from Shouchun in Jiujiang.[20] When he was young he studied in Chang'an and learned the *Ancient Docu-ments*[21] and the *Guliang Spring and Autumn Annals*.[22] He became a prefectural educational official and was deputized as the commandant of Nancheng.

In those days Emperor Cheng [r. 33–7 B.C.E.] had appointed Wang Feng commander in chief of the armed forces. The Wang family mo-nopolized power and ran the court, and though disasters and abnor-malities repeatedly occurred, none of the subordinates dared to speak straightforwardly. Fu submitted three letters emphatically declaring the reasons for the gains and losses of the Qin and Han dynasties, set-ting forth a *Song of the Tenth Month*, including a warning about the dissolute leisure class.[23] His words were earnest, but they were not accepted above.

19. Sima Qian (ca. 145–90 B.C.E.), commonly considered the father of Chinese histo-riography, was the Grand Historian cited by Zhang Tianyu, the editor of this collec-tion, in his foreword.
20. In Jiangxi.
21. A collection of materials purporting to transmit the heritage of political science of ancient dynasties, included among the so-called Chinese classics, or Confucian classics.
22. A commentary on the *Spring and Autumn Annals*, a Confucian classic chroni-cling events from 722 to 481 B.C.E.
23. This refers particularly to the excesses of the Wang family, the clan of the empress.

Emperor Cheng had long-lost genealogies, so Fu thought it appropriate to construct three lineages, designating the heritage of Confucius to be descendants of the Yin [Shang dynasty]. He again submitted a letter, deducing from ancient writings, using *Mr. Zuo*,[24] Guliang, and the *Records of Manners*[25] to clarify each other, that the heritage of Confucius should be considered descended from [King] Tang [founder of the Yin/Shang dynasty]. Subsequently the emperor issued a decree appointing the senior descendant of Confucius as Duke Shaohe of Yin.

At this time, Fu stayed home and occupied himself with reading and nurturing nature. When Wang Mang took over the government,[26] one day Fu left his wife and children and went to Jiujiang. Even today legend makes him out to be an immortal. After that someone saw Fu at Huiji, using a different name, working as a city gate sentry in Wu.

There is a shrine to him in Fengcheng prefecture of Hong province, on the north shore of the great river. It is called the Temple of the Ascended Immortal. In the Shaoxing era [1131–1161] of the Song dynasty he was entitled Officer-Recluse in the Spring of Life, a Realized Human Being.

Taoist Scholarship

BAN SI

Ban Si studied together with his cousin Biao. The family had an endowment of books and a sufficiency of financial resources within itself. Antiquarians from afar would come there; everyone from his father's crony Yang Ziyun[27] on down went to their house.

---

24. A collection of chronicles of the Spring and Autumn era, complementary to the *Spring and Autumn Annals*, differing significantly in content and extent of coverage.
25. Part of the *Classic of Manners*, previously noted as one of the Confucian classics, dealing with the customs and rituals of the Zhou dynasty.
26. In 9 C.E. the regent Wang Mang usurped the throne of the Han dynasty, which was already more than two hundred years old. Wang declared a new dynasty, which he named the Xin, literally meaning "new." He attempted to institute economic and administrative reforms but was opposed by entrenched interests and killed in a civil war in 23 C.E. The Han regime was subsequently reestablished, to reign for another two hundred years.
27. Yang Ziyun was Yang Xiong.

While Si cultivated Confucian studies, he valued the arts of Lao-tzu and Chuang-tzu. When Huan Tan[28] wanted to borrow the book of Chuang-tzu, Si replied, "If you're talking about Chuang-tzu, he stopped being intellectual, abandoned knowledge, cultivated life, and preserved reality, pure and empty, tranquil and calm, attributing it to nature, taking only Creation for his teacher and companion, not compelled by worldly customs.

"Fish in one valley, and myriad beings won't interfere with your will; stay on one hill, and the world will not alter your happiness. Don't get caught in the net of sages, don't sniff the bait of arrogant rulers, don't affirm selfish ambitions. Rhetoricians cannot name this; that is why it is valuable.

"Now you are already completely bound up in benevolence and righteousness, chained to rumor and reputation, following the tracks of the Duke of Zhou[29] and Confucius, running for what was reached by Yan and Min.[30] You're already bound up in secular doctrines—what do you want with the Great Way, to dazzle yourself?

"In ancient times there were those who went to Handan to learn the way the people there walk. They never learned to emulate it, but in the process of trying to imitate the walk of Handan they'd forgotten their former way of walking, so they'd come crawling back home on their hands and knees. I'm afraid you might be like this type, so I'm not going to give you the book."

Taoist Arts

YAN CUN

Yan Cun was styled Junping. He was a man of Shu.[31] He was refined and tranquil and extraordinarily subtle in his scholarship, particularly expert in the *I Ching* and immersed in Lao-tzu and Chuang-tzu.

---

28. Ca. 43 B.C.E.–28 C.E. A scholar and critic who served as a senior official of the regime of Wang Mang.

29. The Duke of Zhou, a Confucian ideal, is portrayed as the principal cultural architect of the Zhou dynasty.

30. Disciples of Confucius.

31. Sichuan. Mount Emei is located in Shu, and this ethnically diverse region has been an important center of much Taoist activity over the centuries, including the original movement of the Celestial Masters. Emei is also an important Buddhist site, said to be the abode of the supernal bodhisattva Guanyin, the epitome of compassion.

He used to practice fortune-telling in the market of Chengdu,[32] reasoning that "fortune-telling is a lowly occupation, but it can be used to benefit many people. When there are perverse and dishonest questions, then I use the medium of auguries to tell them what is beneficial and what is harmful. When speaking to someone's son, I base it on respect; when speaking to someone's younger brother, I base it on accord; when speaking to someone's servant, I base it on loyalty. In each case I lead them to good on the basis of conditions, so more than half follow my advice."

He would only interview a few people a day; then when he'd obtained a hundred coins, enough to sustain himself, he'd close up shop, lower the blinds, and teach *Lao-tzu*. He had read everything and wrote a book of more than a hundred thousand words based on the teachings of Lao-tzu and Chuang-tzu. Yang Xiong studied with him in his youth and attained a lot of Junping's Way.

There was a rich man of Shu named Luo Chong who asked Junping, "Why don't you serve in government?"

Junping said, "No way to express myself."

Chong supplied Junping with carriage, horses, clothing, and food. Junping said, "I am ill, that's all; it's not that I don't have enough. I have a surplus, whereas you don't have enough. How can one who is lacking offer anything to one with a surplus?"

Chong said, "I have ten thousand pieces of gold, while you don't have a pittance. Yet you say you have a surplus. Aren't you mistaken?"

Junping said, "No. I've spent the night at your house before, and you keep working after everyone has gone to bed, busy day and night, never satisfied. Now, I make a living by fortune-telling, and the cash comes to me by itself, without my having to get off my couch. I still have hundreds of coins gathering dust that I don't know what to do with. So is it not the case that I have a surplus whereas you don't have enough?"

Chong was very embarrassed. Junping sighed and said, "What increases our possessions diminishes our spirit; what gives birth to our fame deals death to our body." So after all he didn't serve in government. He finally died, still working, when he was more than ninety

32. The capital city of Shu.

years old. The people of Shu respected and loved him and praise him to this day.

There is a shrine to him in the Cotton Bamboo district of Han province. In the Shaoxing era [1131–1161] of the Song dynasty, Junping was entitled Realized Human Being with Subtle Perceptions.

A Taoist Recluse

ZHENG PU

Zheng Pu was styled Zizhen. He lived in seclusion in Gukou.[33] Keeping to the Way in mystic silence, he practiced the conduct of supreme virtue. He and Junping both cultivated the Way and preserved themselves; one would not ingest what the other would not ingest, one would not eat what the other would not eat.

In the time of Emperor Cheng,[34] the chief general Wang Feng politely invited him, but he never bent to the end. Master Yang's[35] *Words of Law* praises him for tilling under the crags, never bending his will, while his name reverberated through the capital city.

There is a shrine to him in Hanzhong.

Taoist Scholarship

YANG XIONG

Yang Xiong was styled Ziyun. He was a man of Chengdu in Shu. When he was young he was poor, but he admired the Way and read everything he could find. He was quiet and often deep in thought. Pure and unambitious, he had few desires. He did not strive for wealth and status, yet he was not silent in penury and lowliness, and he did not cultivate puritanical fastidiousness for a reputation in his time.

He had a great capacity by nature and didn't like any books but those of sages and savants. If not so inclined, he didn't do anything, even for wealth or status. He wrote books such as *The Great Mystery*

---

33. In Shaanxi.
34. Of the Han dynasty, r. 33 B.C.E.–7 C.E.
35. This refers to the aforementioned Yang Xiong (Yang Ziyun), subject of the next story.

and *Words of Law*, all of them investigating the ultimate meaning of heaven and humanity. He was a famous scholar of the Han dynasty.

His learning was based on Lao-tzu, as can be seen in his writings. For example, "Stillness and silence are the house to safeguard virtue; purity and calm are the garden where the spirit may roam." In *The Great Mystery* he says, "Conceal the mind in the depths, improve the spiritual roots." In *Reckonings* he says, "Concealing the mind in the depths means the spirit doesn't go outside." These all embody the teachings of Lao-tzu.

Taoist Character

THE THREE MAO MASTERS

The elder master's posthumous name was Rong; he was styled Shu Shen. The middle master's posthumous name was Gu; he was styled Jiwei. The younger master's posthumous name was Zhong; he was styled Sihe. They were men of Nanguan in Xianyang.[36]

The elder master was born in 145 B.C.E., the other two brothers were born in 143 B.C.E. and 141 B.C.E. When the elder master was eighteen years old, he left his home and family and went up into Mount Heng[37] and read the *Tao Te Ching* and the "Traditions" of the *I Ching*, meditating and seeking the Way.

Then he went to West City,[38] where he experienced a meeting with Lord Wang, president of the realized people,[39] who put him in charge of vestments, books, and charts. He subsequently attained the Way and became a disciple of the president of the realized people.

When he returned to his home, he was forty-nine years old. He was able to raise the dead and restore them to life; his parents marveled at him in their hearts. He took care of his father and mother until they died, remaining at home for fifty-three years.

The middle master was considered for *filial piety and integrity* in

36. In Shaanxi.
37. In Hunan, one of the five sacred mountains of China.
38. West City Mountain Grotto is the third of the Ten Great Grotto Heavens of Taoism. There is a West City prefecture in Shaanxi, but the exact location of the grotto is said to be unknown. (*Fangyu daolu*, p. 441)
39. An account of this figure can be found in the *Yunji qiqian*, 12. Cf. *Daozang jiyao*, vol. 20, p. 8877a.

the time of Emperor Jing [r. 156–140 B.C.E.], recommended in the category of *wise and good* in 128 B.C.E., and appointed to the rank of court gentleman for miscellaneous functions. In 91 B.C.E. he was transferred to the post of tutor of the crown prince. In 80 B.C.E. he was appointed Commandant to Defeat the Hu[40] and governor of Wuwei.

The youngest master was famous for disciplined conduct in youth. He lived in seclusion in the mountains south of Huashan. In 138 B.C.E., during Emperor Wu's reign, he was recommended in the category *correct and upright*, but he didn't accept it. He moved to the state of Liang, where he was an honored guest of King Xiao. In 68 B.C.E., when Emperor Xuan was on the throne, he was transferred to the post of magistrate of Loyang, then commandant of Xicheng and governor-general of Shangjun. When Emperor Yuan succeeded to the throne [in 48 B.C.E.], he was appointed elder grandee and transferred to the post of governor-general of Xihe.

At that time the middle master was the chamberlain for the imperial insignia and official attendant, with hundreds of local people seeing him off. The elder master said to guests, "Though I am not a minister with a salary of two thousand piculs, still I will have a spiritual post, selected by the Emperor of Heaven to assist the prime minister of the East Mountain, the Lord of Destiny of the Forests of Mount Heng, who is responsible for selecting students of the Way, in charge of the records of life and death for Wu and Yue. This too is a critical position in the spiritual government of the clan leaders of higher reality. On the third day of the fourth month of the coming year I will ascend; will you be able to come to see me as you have today? If any of you come to see me, you don't need to spend anything; I'll provide for you."

When the appointed time came, a welcoming official actually descended, and so the elder master bade final farewell to his clan and family. He said to the local youth, "When I leave here, I'll stay temporarily on Juqu Mountain east of the river. Even though Jiwei and Sihe will be late to see things, they'll surely be able to repent, give up their offices and emoluments, and come looking for me." When he finished speaking, he thanked the people of the time and left.

---

40. Hu is a generic term referring to a number of central Asian peoples.

This took place in 44 B.C.E., when the master was 102 years old. His two younger brothers were still in office. When they heard that their elder brother had attained spiritual immortality in broad daylight, they both gave up their offices and returned home. In 39 B.C.E. they crossed the river to look for their brother in the mountains to the east. When they found him, they wept with sorrow and joy.

The master said to his two younger brothers, "Why were you so late to awaken?" Then after that he gave them miraculous methods of spiritual relief to liberate them, and both became realized people, managing caves of Mount Juqu with a golden altar to the sky south of Huashan. Subsequently the middle master became the Spiritual Lord Determining Records, while the younger master became the Immortal Lord Preserving Destiny. Both are divine offices.

In the year 1 B.C.E., when the elder master was 145 years old, he received nine divinely revealed documents on jade strips and was assigned to the government and jade grotto of Red City in the rank of exalted prefect in charge of destiny, senior minister of Taishan, the Realized Human of the Element Red.

The master told his two younger brothers, "From now on I have official responsibilities, so I can't be coming and going repeatedly. I will come back to this mountain in a year. On the eighteenth day of the third month and the second day of the twelfth month, I plan to ask my teachers, Lord President of Realized People and the Realized Man of Red of the Sky of Mount Heng, to go have a look at your place. You should remember this. If any inclined to the Way await me on those days, I will take care of them myself, having the means to teach those who have not yet understood."

Now the two younger brothers stayed to govern inside the caves of Maoshan, building a temple outside, using the Way in their contact with all beings and all things, distributing benefit to humanity, their generosity extending to birds and beasts, winning the affection of each. With miraculous curses and blessings, crimes and evils invariably came to light.

As their esoteric teachings were enlightened, they were easygoing with exoteric doctrines. Thus the wind and rain were timely, the five grains ripened completely, epidemics did not occur, violence was not committed; there were no disasters in the region, no plundering armies in the towns. The elders of the time sang a song:

Maoshan links to Jinling,
Rivers and lakes occupying downstream.
Three spirits ride white snow geese;
Each one manages a mountain peak.
They summon rain to water dry rice plants;
The fields again turn soft.
Our wives and children all protect our homes,
Letting us be free of worries.
When the white geese have flown into the blue sky,
When will they ever return?

The three masters in the past mounted three places where white snow geese gathered on the mountain, and people of the time saw them, thus giving rise to this song. And also because they were places snow geese gathered, they divided Juqu Mountain into three, the mountain of Elder Master Mao, Middle Master Mao, and Younger Master Mao, respectively. Collectively they're all just one mountain, that is Juqu; there is no other name.

[4]

EASTERN HAN DYNASTY
(25–220)

Taoist Character

ZHANG LING

Zhang Ling (Taoist books avoid his name Daoling) was styled Fu. He was a man from Feng county in Bei province of Han. He was born on Mount Tianmu in Yuhang.

He was originally a college student, widely read in the Five Classics. Late in life he lamented, "This adds nothing to life span." Subsequently he studied the Yellow Emperor's *Nine Cauldron Alchemy Scripture*.[1] The elixir was made on Mount Fan Yang. He also found a concealed book in a cave on Mount Song.

At that time China was in chaos, with the Han dynasty in decline. Realizing that the pursuit of literature was withering and dying and inadequate to get out of danger and help the world, he retired into seclusion in Yuhang for ten years. Then he went with his disciples into Shu.

The peasants of Shu gathered in droves, serving him as their teacher. He used only integrity, honor, kindness, and mercy to sway the people, not liking to use punishments and penalties. Anyone who had an illness was required to set forth his sins and promise to God, on pain of death, to mend his ways.

---

1. The number nine is associated with pure yang, or pure positive energy, and consequently features in the titles of many esoteric texts. The goal of Taoist immortalism is sometimes expressed in terms of converting all the energy of the body-mind into pure positive energy. Nine is also represented as the sum of the four cardinal directions, the four intermediate directions, and the center; the eight trigrams of the *I Ching* are arrayed around a circle in the eight directions, while the consciousness of the practitioner is stabilized in the center of the circle.

He opened a salt spring for the benefit of the people, chased off giant serpents, and warred on demons,[2] inflicting twenty-four defeats and making twenty-four jurisdictions,[3] getting rid of pests of the people of Shu. Having practiced all the arts of controlling and commanding the mountain spirits, his achievements and his virtues both outstanding, he was called a Celestial Teacher.[4] The ones who thoroughly mastered his Way were disciples Wang Chang and Zhao Sheng.[5]

A Taoist Recluse

XIANG CHANG

Xiang Chang was styled Ziping. He was a man from Chaoge, east of the Yellow River.[6] He secluded himself at home; by nature he valued balance and harmony and was fond of the *Tao Te Ching* and the *I Ching*.

Once, as he was reading the *I Ching*, coming to the hexagrams Decrease and Increase,[7] he sighed, "I already realize that riches are not as good as poverty and prestige is not as good as lowliness, but I don't know how life compares to death."

He was poor, without means of support. Benefactors used to take turns providing him with food; he accepted it, taking what he needed and returning the rest.

---

2. According to an essay in the Buddhist collection *Hongmingji*, this term *demon* did not refer to supernatural beings but was an uncomplimentary reference to non-Han peoples. This usage does have a precedent in the *I Ching*, and it would also help to explain the willingness of the Chinese secular authorities to enfranchise the Celestial Masters cult politically.

3. For the twenty-four jurisdictions, see *Yunji qiqian* 6, *Daozang jiyao*, vol. 19, pp. 8640–44.

4. *Tianshi*. This marks the founding of the Tianshidao, or Way of the Celestial Teachers. For the establishment of this cult as a secular power under Zhang Daoling's grandson Zhang Lu, see *Sanguozhi* 8.

5. It may be noteworthy that this account does not mention hereditary succession in this path. For accounts of the disciples Wang Chang and Zhao Sheng, see the *Longhushanzhi* 7 (Qing dynasty version). This latter-day collection, *Records of Dragon and Tiger Mountain*, contains a more expansive account of Zhang Daoling and his school, including both hereditary and nonhereditary successions.

6. In Henan.

7. Nos. 41 and 42, respectively. These symbols function as a pair. An appendix of the *I Ching* says, "Decrease and increase are the beginnings of strength and debility."

During the Jianwu era [25–56 C.E.], once his sons and daughters were married, he carefully terminated his family affairs and went to roam the five sacred mountains with a free mind. It is not known where he died.

Taoist Influence

FENG PENG

Feng Peng was styled Ziqing. He was a man of Doushang in the North Sea region.[8] When he heard Wang Mang[9] had killed his own son, Yu, he said to friends, "Social order has been disrupted; if I don't leave, trouble will extend to others." Then he resigned from office, took his family to sea, and took up temporary residence in Liaodong.

Peng was an expert in Yin-Yang and knew Wang Mang was going to be defeated; carrying a clay jug on his head, he wailed in the market-place, "A New dynasty? A New dynasty?"[10] Accordingly, he subsequently disappeared and went into hiding.

Then when Emperor Guangwu ascended the throne [in 25 C.E.],[11] Peng went to Luoshan in Langye, developing his will and practicing the Way. Everyone was influenced by his virtue. He was repeatedly summoned by the emperor for court service, but he never budged, so he lived out his natural life span.

Taoist Recluses

YAN GUANG

Yan Guang was styled Ziling. He was a man of Yuchao in Huiji. When young he had a lofty reputation and was a fellow student with the future emperor Guangwu.

When Guangwu became emperor, Yan Guang changed his name and disappeared.

---

8. On the Shandong peninsula.

9. That is, the usurper of the throne of Han.

10. As noted earlier, Wang Mang named his regime the Xin, or New, dynasty.

11. Emperor Guangwu of Han lived from 5 B.C.E. to 57 C.E. and reigned from 25 to 57 C.E. His rule marks a restoration of the Han dynasty after the overthrow of Wang Mang's New dynasty.

The emperor, considering his wisdom, ordered that a search be made for him. Eventually a report submitted from the state of Qi said, "There is a man who dresses in sheepskin and fishes in the swamps."

The emperor suspected it was Guang, so he had a comfortable carriage and gifts prepared and sent an emissary to invite him to court.

It took three trips before he finally came, and then he lodged with the army.

Guang just lay there and didn't get up. The emperor went to where he lay, patted Guang on the stomach, and said, "Tut, tut, Ziling! Can't you help me govern?"

Guang went back to sleep without answering. After a while he opened his eyes wide and stared. He said, "In ancient times Yao and Shun revealed their virtue, but Chao Fu just washed his ears. A gentleman certainly has an aspiration—why should he be pressed?"

The emperor said, "After all, I can't subordinate you, can I?" With this, he got into his carriage, sighed, and left.

Another time, he brought Guang to the palace and talked of old times, conversing for days. The emperor casually asked Guang, "How do I compare with the past?"

He replied, "Your Majesty's errors are more than before."

As they were reclining, Guang put his foot on the emperor's midriff. The next day, the chief astrologer reported that an irregular star had seriously intruded upon the imperial constellation. The emperor laughed and said, "My old friend Yan Ziling was reclining with me, that's all." His minister of education, Hou Bo, wrote in a letter, "Embrace benevolence, foster justice, and the world will rejoice; if obedience to order is only flattery, essential command is cut off."

Guang was appointed grand master of remonstrance, but he wouldn't accept. Instead he farmed on Mount Fuchun.[12] Later, people named the place where he fished Yan Ling's Shallows. In 41 C.E. he was again specially summoned by the emperor, but he didn't go. He died at home at the age of eighty. The emperor sorely missed him.

LIANG HONG

Liang Hong was styled Boluan. He was a man of Pingling in Fufeng.[13] His family was poor, and he herded pigs.

12. In Zhejiang.
13. In Shaanxi.

Once he accidentally let fire get out of control and it burned some-one's house. Hong recompensed the owner with all of his pigs, but the owner still considered that insufficient. So Hong asked if he could work off the rest himself as an indentured servant.

Later, when he returned to his native village, influential families admired his lofty integrity, and many wanted to marry their daugh-ters to him, but Hong declined them all.

A certain Mr. Meng of the same district had a daughter who was fat, ugly, and dark, strong enough to lift a stone mortar. Choosy about a mate, she still hadn't married by the time she was thirty. When her par-ents asked her why, she said, "I want to find a sage like Liang Boluan."

When Liang heard of this, he sent her an invitation.

The woman usually wore muslin clothes and hempen shoes and kept her spinning tools in a woven basket. But then when she wed, at first she entered the home all dressed up. Hong didn't speak to her for seven days. Finally she knelt at the foot of the bed and said, "I heard you were high-minded and righteous and had refused numerous brides. I too have refused numerous husbands. Now that I have been selected, I presume I don't deserve to be mistreated."

Hong said, "I wanted someone in coarse wool and leather who could live in seclusion with me deep in the mountains. Now here you are in gorgeous silks, wearing makeup and mascara. Is this my desire?"

His wife said, "This is just to see what your intention is, that's all. I have my own clothes for living in seclusion." Then she redid her hair into mallet buns, put on cotton clothes, and set about doing chores.

Hong was overjoyed. "This is truly the wife for Liang Hong! You can be a companion to me!" He styled her Deyao, "Resplendent with Virtue."

They went together into the mountains of Baling and made a liv-ing farming and weaving. He recited the classics of poetry and history and played the lute as a hobby. Admiring the high-minded men of earlier ages, he wrote eulogies of twenty-four men since the Four Elders.[14]

---

14. See the account of Zhang Liang. The Four Elders were savants consulted to settle a succession crisis in the imperial house in the early Han dynasty. References to these savants appear repeatedly in subsequent history, representing a positive rela-tionship between the imperial cultus and the wizards of the mountains.

On his way east, he passed the capital city and wrote "A Song of Five Sighs":

> I climb that northern waste—sigh—
> Wanting to see the imperial capital—sigh.
> The palace buildings are huge—sigh—
> The people's labor is tiring—sigh—
> It goes on and on, and still not done—sigh!

The emperor heard of this and condemned it. He instituted a search for Hong but didn't find him.

Hong then changed his surname to Yunqi, his given name to Yao, and his style to Houguang. He stayed with his wife and children between the states of Yan and Qi, then left and went to Wu, where he lived under the eaves of the house of a rich man, Hao Botong, working for people as a hired rice pounder. Every time he returned, his wife would have food for him. She did not presume to look up in Hong's presence but held the tray up to the level of her eyebrows. When Botong witnessed this, he marveled at it. "If that laborer can get his wife to respect him like that," he said, "he is not an ordinary man." Only then did he lodge them in his house.

When Hong was sick and suffering, he said to his host, "Please don't let my son observe the rites of mourning." When he died, Botong and others looked for a place to bury him next to the tomb of Wu Yaoli. They agreed: "Yaoli was a man of mettle, and Boluan was pure and high-minded; they should be near each other."

Hong was a friend of Gao Hui.

Gao Hui

Gao Hui was styled Botong. He was a man of the capital city. He was fond of the *Lao-tzu* and lived in seclusion in the mountains south of Huashan. He was a good friend of Liang Hong's.

When Hong traveled east, he missed Hui and wrote a poem saying:

> Birds call to each other,
> An invitation to companionship.
> Thinking of Master Gao, I have my memories;
> As I'm remembering Hui, they gather together here.

The two never met again.

Hui also conscientiously refused to work for the government all of his life.

Taoist Character

WEI BOYANG

Wei Boyang was a man of Wu. Born a son of an eminent family, he had a natural inclination to Taoist arts and would not work in government. He lived quietly and nurtured nature. None of his contemporaries knew where he was coming from; they thought he was just managing his people and taking care of himself.

He went into the mountains and made spiritual elixir. When it was done, he took it, died, and came back to life. He and his disciple surnamed Yu both became immortal and left. On the road they met a woodcutter, to whom Boyang entrusted a letter of farewell to the people of his hometown and to two disciples.

Boyang wrote *Triplex Unity*[15] and *Analogies of the Five Elements* in three volumes. The rhetoric resembles the *I Ching,* but in reality it borrows the hexagram images to discuss the meaning of the great elixir. But people of the world don't consider alchemical matters and mostly interpret this in terms of yin and yang, missing the essential message.

As for the book *Triplex Unity,* the great Confucians Zhu Yuanhui and Zhan Yuanding both drew deeply on its principles and often touched upon it in their debates. No one can see into it without clear understanding of the deep meanings of the *I Ching* and the *Tao Te Ching.*

Taoist Recluses

TAI TONG

Tai Tong was styled Xiaowei. He was a man of Ye in Wei prefecture.[16] He lived in seclusion on Mount Wu'an,[17] where he excavated a cave to dwell in and gathered herbs to support himself.

The regional inspector making his rounds had a functionary pay

15. Cf. *Daozang jiyao,* vols. 10 and 11 for texts and commentaries.
16. In Henan.
17. In Hebei.

him a visit, but Tong refused on a pretext of illness. The regional inspector then went in person with a gift to see Tong. He asked him, "Why do you keep yourself in such misery?"

Tong said, "I am fortunate to be able to preserve my natural life to the end, maintaining my spirit and nurturing harmony. Wouldn't it be more painful to work for a ruler by day promulgating decrees, while worrying about everything at night?"

After that he disappeared, never to be seen again.

HAN KANG

Han Kang was styled Boxiu, also named Dianxiu. He was a man of the Boling district of the capital, from a distinguished lineage. For more than thirty years he gathered herbs on famous mountains and sold them in the market of Chang'an, never quoting two prices.

Once when a girl was buying medicine from Kang, he stuck to his price and wouldn't move. The girl angrily said, "You're Han Boxiu, aren't you? And you won't come down in price?"

Kang lamented, "I originally wanted to avoid fame, but now even little girls know me! What's the use of medicine?" Then he fled into the mountains of Boling.

Taoist Silence

JIAO ZHEN

Jiao Zhen was styled Zhongyan. He was a man of Moling in Fufeng. When he was young he was attracted to Huang-Lao;[18] disappearing into mountain valleys, he lived in caves and aspired to the energy-induction arts of the Master of the Red Pines[19] and Wang Zijiao.[20]

He was a hometown contemporary of Ma Rong[21] and Su Zhang,[22] both of whom gave him precedence. Wu Cang of Runan respected him very much, and so sent him a letter to see his will:

18. I.e. Taoism, particularly of the type represented by texts associated with Huangdi (the Yellow Emperor) and Lao-tzu, reputed author of the *Tao Te Ching*.
19. Cf. *Yunji qiqian 8, Daozang jiyao*, vol. 20, p. 8684.
20. Cf. *Yunji qiqian 8, Daozang jiyao*, vol. 20, pp. 8686–88.
21. Lived from 79 to 166. Ma Rong was a famous scholar, noted for commentaries on the Five Classics.
22. Su Zhang was a magistrate noted for integrity in office.

"Zhongyan diligently keeps to seclusion and austerity. While those who ride on the clouds and those who go through the mud do not lodge in the same abode, whenever there is a west wind, I always sigh in lament. I've heard that the sayings of Huang and Lao ride the void into the unknown, concealing the person in remote detachment, yet there is also running countries and taking care of people, applicable to government administration. When it comes to climbing mountains and obliterating tracks, the spirits do not reveal their testimony, people do not see the results.

"I seek from you what you approve; what is your opinion? In ancient times Officer Yin[23] refrained from embracing the Way to await a ruler like Yao or Shun.[24] The present time is enlightened, the four seas are open; Chao and Xu have no purpose for Basket Mountain,[25] Yi and Qi would regret going into Shouyang.[26] If you can really ride dragons and sport with phoenixes, soaring among the clouds, then this is nothing foxes and rabbits or swallows and sparrows can figure out."

Zhen didn't reply.

23. A savant who advised King Tang, founder of the Shang (Yin) dynasty in the late eighteenth century B.C.E. According to tradition, he originally supported himself by tilling the soil, but Tang requested his help three times, and he finally agreed to advise him.

24. Yao and Shun are commonly cited as archetypes of idealized sage rulers of predynastic times.

25. Chao and Xu refer to Chao Fu and Xu You, archetypes of men of wisdom who conscientiously avoided involvement in government. When Chao Fu was offered the throne by the sage king Shun, he went and washed out his ears in the river. When Xu You heard of this, he led his ox upstream to drink. Basket Mountain refers to retirement from the world of affairs.

26. Yi and Qi refer to Bo Yi and Shu Qi, brothers who abandoned their fief at the end of the Shang dynasty three thousand years ago. At first they deferred to each other, then relinquished all of their patrimony after the jurisdiction of the Shang dynasty granting their land rights had been taken over by the state of Zhou. They are commonly cited as models of personal integrity, though the principle implicated may be interpreted differently according to context. They were not ejected from their lands by the Zhou dynasty but refused to contract with Zhou, voluntarily renouncing their domain, so their conduct is typically viewed individually, apart from traditional stereotypes of Zhou and Shang. Shouyang refers to the mountains where they starved to death after "refusing to eat the grain of Zhou." In Chan Buddhism, these brothers are cited to represent arhats who remain in nirvana and refuse to return to the world to practice compassion after becoming personally liberated. A Chan proverb states, "If you understand, you will return to your village and become a rustic; if you don't understand, you will starve to death on Shouyang."

He lived to be more than seventy years old but would never marry. He subsequently returned to his home all of a sudden, announced the day of his death, and actually passed away at the appointed time.

Later people saw Zhen in Dunhuang, so those of the earlier generation considered him extraordinary.

A Taoist Recluse

FA ZHEN

Fa Zhen was styled Guoqing. He was a man of Mei in Fufeng. He was fond of study but had no permanent home. He had broad mastery of inner and outer charts[27] and classics; he was a great scholar of Guanxi, with hundreds of disciples coming from afar.

He was taciturn by nature and had few desires. He didn't get involved in societal affairs. When the governor-general asked to meet him, he went to call on him wearing a simple head cloth.[28] The governor-general wanted to retain him in the Labor Section, but Zhen said, "Your Honor is being treated with courtesy, so you presume to coerce conformity with yourself. If you try to make an official out of me, I'll be south of the southernmost mountains, north of the northernmost mountains."

Tian Rao of the same prefecture recommended Zhen in these terms: "He personally does the work of all four classes, lives in obscurity, peaceful and calm, trying to walk in the lofty footsteps of Lao-tzu, not bending to material inducements. I wish the imperial court would give him a job in civil service; he would surely be able to play the song of Purifying the Shrine and attract the manner-correcting phoenixes."

27. Charts are schematic sets of symbols, ideas, deities, demons, doctrines, and directions. They may be compared to Buddhist *yantras* and mandalas and were to become increasingly prominent in Taoism as Buddhism spread in China. *Inner and outer* typically refers to esoteric and exoteric lore, but its application can be extended. In this context, it could refer to Taoist (inner) and Confucian (outer), or Chinese (inner) and Buddhist (outer). In Chinese Buddhist literature, *inner and outer* commonly means spiritual and secular, or Buddhist and Confucian.
28. That is to say, in the fashion of a hermit.

The emperor humbly tried to get him to come to court, summoning him four times altogether. Zhen said, "Since I can't disappear from the world, how can I drink water in which ears have been washed?" Subsequently he secluded himself completely. His friend Guo Zheng praised him, "Fa Zhen's name may be heard, but he's hard to meet in person. He fled fame, yet fame followed him; he avoided repute, but repute pursued him. He can be called teacher of a hundred generations!" They had a eulogy to him inscribed in stone, referring to him as the Master of Mystic Virtue.

Taoism and Government

Liu Kuan

Liu Kuan was styled Wenrao. He was a man of Hongnong.[29] He lived to be seventy-three years old. One day he met the Master of Green Valley,[30] who descended into his bedroom and taught him the method of turning into a staff to be liberated.[31] He took him off into Huashan to practice nine breaths to take in energy and also taught him a method of furnace-fire alchemy. Liu Kuan practiced them and after completing the course came to a grotto on Huashan, where he was in charge of beginners in the study of the Way.

Kuan served the government of the Han dynasty, reaching the rank of commandant in the Ministry of Education and Civil affairs. He was fond of practicing hidden charity, rescuing the poor and needy. The populace was pleased, and people felt as close to him as to their own parents.

29. In Henan.

30. This character is cited in *Legends of Immortals of the Grottoes* 2, according to which it was not known where he was from. No other identifying marks, such as his name, are recorded. He is said to have practiced the breathing exercises mentioned here and subsequently compounded an alchemical elixir, which he then ingested, attaining the Way. This latter account says he descended from heaven to meet Liu Kuan. This story is one of those that prefigure the esotericism that would become characteristic of Taoist grotto cults like the Maoshan path.

31. This seems to refer to the practice of leaving behind a staff in place of the corpse when disappearing to die.

A Taoist Recluse

MR. PANG

Mr. Pang was a man of Xiangyang in Nanjun.[32] He lived south of Xianshan[33] and never once went into the city. He and his wife were as respectful to each other as to guests.

The inspector of the Jing region, Liu Biao, sent numerous invitations but could not successfully importune him, so he himself went to visit him. He said to him, "How can keeping one body intact compare to keeping the empire intact?"

Mr. Pang laughed and said, "Snow geese nest in the high forests; come evening, they find their place to rest. Tortoises and crocodiles have their nooks on the floor of deep waters; at night they find their place to stay. Now then, moral and practical choices are men's nests and nooks; each finds his place to abide, that's all."

As he was tilling on a hilltop, with his wife and children hoeing in front of him, Biao pointed and asked, "You are living in hardship in the fields, unwilling to accept office and salary. What will you leave your heirs when you pass on?"

Mr. Pang said, "People of the world all bequeath danger; now I alone bequeath safety to my posterity. Though what I leave is not the same, that doesn't mean I'm not leaving any bequest."

Eventually he climbed Deer Gate Mountain[34] with his wife and children. There they gathered herbs and never returned.

A Taoist Scholar

LIAO FU

Liao Fu was styled Wenqi. He was a man of Pingyu in Runan.[35] He studied the Han version of the *Classic of Poetry* and the Ouyang version of *Ancient Documents*.[36] He taught as many as several hundred people.

---

32. In Jiangsu.
33. There are three mountains with this name in Zhejiang.
34. In Hubei.
35. In Henan.
36. This version of the classic *Shang Shu* was lost in the fourth century C.E.

His father was condemned for some incident and died in prison. Influenced by the fact that his father lost his life on account of the law, Fu was wary of becoming an official. When his mourning was done, he lamented, "Lao-tzu has a saying—'Which is dearer, your reputation or your body?' Why should I work for a reputation?" So he cut off his ambitions, beyond the world, and focused exclusively on classics.

He was particularly expert at astronomy and calendography. Attempts were made to recruit him at all levels of government, but he didn't respond to any of them.

When Fu knew the crops were going to be bad, he'd collect large quantities of grain just to help out his clan and his wife's relatives. He also arranged for the interment of those who died in epidemics whose families couldn't take care of them by themselves. People of the time called him the Professor of the Northern Outskirts. When he was eighty years old he died at home.

Taoist Advice

FAN YING

Fan Ying was styled Jiqi. He was a man of Luyang in Nanyang.[37] When he was young he received instruction in the capital; he studied the *I Ching* of Mr. Jing[38] and also learned the Five Classics. He was also skilled at divining by wind direction and astrology as well as the Seven Parallels of the River[39] and Luo diagrams,[40] and predicting disasters and abnormalities. He lived in seclusion north of Pot Mountain[41] and did not respond when the province and prefecture tried to recruit him. He was recommended for civil service examinations in the categories *chief of the wise and good* and *imbued with the Way,* but he didn't go for any of them.

37. In Henan.
38. By the Han dynasty scholar Jing Fang, 77–33 B.C.E.
39. Parallels were a class of esoteric texts purporting to draw hidden meanings from orthodox classics. They are said to have first appeared in the Qin dynasty (third century B.C.E.) and disappeared in the Sui dynasty (sixth century C.E.).
40. These diagrams are schematic arrays of the fundaments of the native Chinese conceptual universe. They are used for various purposes. See *I Ching Mandalas* by Thomas Cleary (1989, 2000) for a syncretic interpretation of their symbolism.
41. In Henan.

In 127 C.E. Emperor Shun [r. 122–144] sent a letter full of courtesies and accompanied by gifts to recruit him. But he stoutly refused, claiming to be very ill. Then the emperor sent an order pressing the authorities of the prefecture and county to convey him to the capital.

Once in the city, Ying wouldn't budge, claiming to be ill. Even when he was brought by force to the palace, he still wouldn't give in. The emperor got angry and said, "I can grant you life and I can kill you. I can elevate you and I can demean you. I can enrich you and I can impoverish you. Why do you disregard my command?"

Ying said, "I received my destiny from heaven. If I live out my destiny, that is due to heaven; if I die without attaining my destiny, that too is due to heaven. How can Your Majesty give me life? How can you kill me?

"I view violent rulers like looking upon enemies; I would not even be willing to stand in their courts. Is it possible to ennoble me? Even though a commoner, I am at ease and self-possessed in poverty and wouldn't trade it for supremacy over a state with ten thousand war chariots. So is it possible to demean me?

"I wouldn't accept an improper emolument even if it were enormous, and I don't mind living on meager fare if I can express my will. How can Your Majesty enrich me, how can you impoverish me?"

The emperor couldn't get him to bend, but he respected his reputation and sent him to the imperial physician to take care of his illness. The emperor ordered the magistrate of gate traffic control to guide, with the secretary of state leading; he presented him with an elbow rest and a staff and treated him with the courtesy due a mentor. Whenever there were portents concerning the court, the emperor would command that Ying be asked how to restore order. What he said was often proven effective.

He lived to be more than seventy years old and died at home.

Taoist Character

WANG YUAN

Wang Yuan was styled Fangping. He was a man of Donghai.[42] He was recommended in the category of *filial and honest* and appointed a

---

42. Meaning "Eastern Sea"; this region included parts of Shandong and Jiangsu.

gentleman of the interior. After a while he was promoted to grand master of court counseling and dealings. He studied widely in the Five Classics and was particularly well versed in astronomy, schematics, prognostication, and the techniques of the River and Luo diagrams. He had foreknowledge of the periods of flourishing and decline of the empire, the good and bad prospects of the nine regions, seeing them as clearly as in the palm of his hand.

Later he quit his office and went into the mountains to cultivate the Way. When he'd attained the Way, Emperor Huan [r. 147–167] summoned him repeatedly, but he would not emerge, so the emperor had the governor of the prefecture bring him to the capital by force. Yuan hung his head, kept his mouth shut, and wouldn't reply to the imperial command. Then he inscribed some four hundred characters on the boards of the door of the gate, all about things to come. The emperor didn't like this and had someone plane it off, but once the characters outside were removed, characters inside appeared; the ink had penetrated the boards.

Fangping had no children or grandchildren; successive generations of local people collaborated in doing chores for him. [Another source says, "Fangping never returned; local people worked for his descendants for generations."]

The former defender in chief of the same prefecture, Chen Dan, built a House of Tao for Fangping and paid respects to him morning and night, but he only begged for enrichment and elimination of troubles, he didn't study the Way with him. [Another source says, "He begged to learn the Way from him."]

Fangping stayed in Dan's house for more than forty years. Then he said, "My allotted time is almost up; I must go, I cannot stay anymore. I'll set off tomorrow at midday." When the time arrived, Fangping died.

Dan knew he had gone by sublimation, so he didn't dare inter him. He just wept sadly and said in lament, "Have you gone, leaving me? What's to become of me?" He prepared a casket, burned incense, and laid him out fully clothed on the bed.

On the third night of the third day, the corpse disappeared. The sash of his robe had not been untied; it was as if a snake had shed its skin.

A hundred and some days after Fangping left, Dan also died. Some say Dan attained Fangping's Way and left by sublimation. Some say

Fangping left because he knew Dan was about to die and so he abandoned him.

Later, as Fangping passed through Wu on his way east to Guaizang, he stayed in the house of Cai Jing of Xumen. Jing was a commoner, but his bones and features corresponded to those of immortals; that is why Fangping went to his house.

As he was talking to Jing, he said, "It is your destiny in life to succeed in transcending the world, but you didn't learn the Way when young, so now you are more physical than ethereal and should only pursue liberation from the corpse. Liberation from the corpse is very difficult; you simply have to do it like pulling a dog through a hole."[43] Giving him essential advice, he left Jing and departed.

Later, Jing actually molted like a cicada and disappeared. Gone for more than ten years, he suddenly returned home. He said to his family, "On the seventh day of the seventh month, Master Wang will come passing through. That day you should prepare several hundred containers of food and drink to provide for the accompanying officials." Then he left.

On the indicated day Fangping did actually come, leading followers with a signal pennant, his manner dashing as a great general's. He had a rendezvous with Ma Gu at Jing's house.

A neighbor, Chen Wei, kowtowed and begged to be allowed to pay respects. He wanted to acquire masterhood comparable to Cai Jing's. Fangping said, "Get up and stand in the sunlight." Looking at him from behind, Fangping said, "Oh! Your heart is not upright; your shadow is not straight. You can never be taught the Way of immortals. I will give you a job of masterhood on earth."

When Fangping was about to leave, he put a talisman and a key to its code in a small box and handed it to Chen Wei, saying it could be used to relieve disasters and quell demons. Chen Wei subsequently lived to be 110 years old.

He once received a gift of calligraphy from Fangping. The calligraphy was carefree, large, and not ornate. Before this no one knew Fangping's name was Yuan. This information was related by Chen Wei.

---

43. This refers to exiting the body through the nirvana opening in the head. The advanced Taoist practice called projecting the spirit can be considered a preparation for this liberation from the corpse, eliminating the sense of physicality in dying, easing the difficulty mentioned here. See the end of the story of Han Chong.

Taoist Influence

HAN CHONG

Han Chong was styled Changji. He was a man of Biling in Wu prefecture.[44] When he was young he liked the Way. Wang Weixuan, immortal of the Forest House,[45] had taught him a formula for mercury elixir, which Chong carried out carefully, with great results. Weixuan said to him, "By practicing this path, you can serve in public office too without any hindrance to ascension to immortality."

Chong subsequently served in office, gradually reaching the post of magistrate of Wanling. He practiced humaneness to administer government and applied the Way to comfort the people. Tigers and wolves stayed away, locusts didn't swarm in the territory.

Transferred to the post of governor of Runan, he promoted Administrative Clerk Yuan An. An later rose in rank to minister of education and civic affairs; people of the time said that Chong had the perceptivity to recognize character.

When Empress Yin was entombed in the capital, the wives of the officials of neighboring prefectures with salaries of two thousand piculs were supposed to gather at the imperial mausoleum. Chong alone lived in pure simplicity, and his wife got mad at him and cried. An imperial missive inquired into the reason. The chamberlain for ceremonials Ping Yi replied:

"The governor of Runan, Han Chong, is a pure ascetic, highly detached; savoring the Way, he forgets his physical body. He holds an important office, yet his wife does her own spinning. His administration is benevolent and uncomplicated, and he looks upon the people with pity. He has profoundly mastered an extraordinarily wide range of learning, and he has the perception of a man with the capacity for leadership. He is a luminous jewel on a dark night; he is Your Majesty's equivalent to Zichan.[46] His wife does not comprehend the discipline of austerity and complains she has nothing to wear. That merely shows Chong's

---

44. In Jiangsu.

45. The Forest House, in Jiangsu, is the name of the ninth of the Ten Great Grotto Heavens of Taoism.

46. Zichan (580–522 B.C.E.) was a grandee of the state of Zheng during the Spring and Autumn era of the Zhou dynasty, famous for engineering economic and administrative reform in his state.

enlightened virtue." The emperor deemed this extraordinary and increased Chong's salary and rank to the level of two thousand piculs.

When the future emperor Ming [r. 227–239] was on a hunting expedition in Runan and commandeered Chong's official residence, Chong had his wife go stay in the house of an old woman who lived alone. When the emperor heard of this, he said in admiration, "Han Chong is what they call one whom a hundred smeltings won't melt down," and bestowed a gift of fifty rolls of heavy silk.

Chong was in the prefecture for a total of fourteen years. His administration was distinguished for harmony, best in the whole empire. When he was seventy-four years old, Weixian taught him a method of liberation by disappearing, and he managed to leave and go into Dahuo Mountain.[47] Weixuan also taught him the art of escaping and sublimating through the purple door of the nirvana center[48] to transcend the world.

Later he became left overseer of the interior in the caves of Huayang. Tao Hongjing[49] said, "The account in the *Book of Han* is generally the same; there is a little variation in the wording, that's all."

Taoist Arts

XIA FU

Xia Fu was styled Zizhi. He was a man of Chenliu.[50] He was attracted to the Way in youth, and he ingested preparations of atractylodes[51] and mica.[52] Later he went into the mountains of Wu and

---

47. In Sichuan.

48. This refers to the *niwan* "aperture" at the top of the head, used in esoteric internal-attention exercises in both Chinese and Indian traditions. *Niwan* is a transliteration of the Sanskrit word *nirvana*, used in early translations of Buddhist texts but subsequently replaced to avoid confusion with the adopted Taoist usage.

49. Compiler and annotator of *Declarations of the Realized*. Also called the Recluse.

50. In Henan.

51. *Bai zhu*, so-called white atractylodes, is perhaps the most mentioned herb in these stories. Various pharmacological actions are attributed to *bai zhu*: increase in digestive juices, promotion of body weight and muscle strength, reduction of blood sugar, antibacterial, anticoagulant, diuretic, and sedative.

52. Various micas contain as many as thirty-seven minerals, including such essential micronutrients as iron, potassium, and magnesium, but in this type of literature it is not specified what type of mica is used and what processing is applied to make the nutrients available for absorption.

learned a method of refining the soul from Master Red Whiskers. He stayed in a grotto of Huayang, where he served as morning attendant gentleman.

When Fu was young, he was summoned to court by the Secretariat. He fastened the document to a mulberry tree and left. This is how high-minded he was.

Tao Hongjing said, "The *Book of Han* and *Stories of Eminent Men* both say Fu was a man of Yu in Chenliu; in the time of Emperor Huan [r. 147–167] he was appointed direct advisor, but he didn't take up the post."

Taoist Influence

LIU YI

Liu Yi was styled Ziyi. The *Book of Han* makes his style Zixiang. Yi was originally a man of Yingchuan.[53] He was devoted to the virtues of the Way from youth, and as his family was very rich, he was always able to provide public assistance without considering it charity. Many were the dead he took care of and the poor he helped out. He was appointed accounts assistant, given the rank of gentleman of the interior, and promoted to the post of governor of Chenliu. He went out within a radius of five hundred *li* from Chang'an, disposing of the dead and helping out the destitute, sacrificing his own to share with others. When he came to Yangping, he happened to meet Master Ma Huang, who told Yi, "Your humaneness moves heaven and earth, your hidden charity moves spirits and ghosts. Taishang is going to celebrate your compassion; he sent me to come guide you on the path of eternal life."

Yi kowtowed and begged to attend him. So he took him into Pawlonia and Cedar Mountain,[54] where he taught him eight techniques of hiding in the earth and a method of internalizing the beams of five stars. On initiation he was named Donghua. Entering the caves of Huayang, he became right-hand supervisor of the interior in the Office of Determining Registry.

53. In Henan.
54. In Henan.

THE ERA OF THE THREE KINGDOMS
(221–265)

A Taoist Scholar

ZHANG CUN

Zhang Cun was styled Ziming. When young he attended college, where he studied both inner and outer doctrines. Gao Gan, governor of Bing province, petitioned that he be appointed magistrate of Laoling, but he wouldn't accept the post. He moved away to Changshan;[1] his students numbered in the hundreds. Cao Cao[2] tried to make him secretary of state, but though he was summoned he did not go.

During the Taihe era [of Wei, 227–239], a decree was issued to find scholars in seclusion. The prefecture repeatedly recommended Cun, and he was sent for, but he didn't go, claiming old age and illness. Three days after Lu Yu, governor-general of Guangping, arrived to take up office, the county recorder announced he was going to deliver a letter to Cun following up, but Yu instructed him, "Master Zhang is one of those who do not serve the emperor above and do not consort with the lords below. How can he be honored by this visit?" He just sent the recorder to deliver an official letter and present gifts of mutton and wine.

When Zhang died he was 105 years old. That year the governor-general Wang Xiao took office; he issued instructions to the counties under his command: "When I was in the capital city previously, I heard of Zhang Ziming; now that I've come here and inquired after

1. This is another name of the sacred Mount Heng.
2. Cao Cao, the powerful warlord of Wei in the Three Kingdoms period, tried to gather as many Taoist wizards as possible, allegedly to keep them under supervision in view of their influence on the people.

him, I find he's already passed away, much to my regret. This man was an earnest scholar who lived in seclusion and did not compete with contemporaries. He comforted himself with the Way. Long ago an old man of Jiangxian stayed humbly in the muddy road, but Zhao Meng[3] raised him up and the lords were friendly to him. Have compassion for the elderly who diligently adhere to the Way but have not been honored or favored. Write to them and send emissaries to ask after their families; put prominent inscriptions over their doors, striving to enhance the sense of distinction, so as to give solace to those who have already gone while encouraging those yet to come."

Taoist Silence

JIAO XIAN

Jiao Xian was styled Xiaoran. He was a man of Hedong.[4] As the Han dynasty came to an end, the heartland was in chaos; Xian lost his whole family, escaping alone to a river islet, eating plants and drinking water, with no clothes or shoes.

At that time Zhu Nan, chief of Taiyang, saw him at a distance and thought he was a refugee and wanted to send a boat to pick him up. Hou Wuyang of the same prefecture told the county authorities he was only a madman, then registered him and gave him a daily allowance of five pints. Everyone was contemptuous of him. Nevertheless, when going about he never trod an improper shortcut but would invariably go along the walkways between the fields. When gleaning, he didn't take the biggest ears of grain; though hungry he never ate to his fill, and though cold he never overdressed. Whenever he went out, if he saw a woman he'd conceal himself, only to emerge after she was gone.

He prepared a cow shed for himself, swept it clean, built a bed of wood and covered it with hay. When the weather was cold, he'd make a fire to warm himself, groaning and talking to himself.

Around the year 230 he took a staff in hand and was going to cross over to the south, but the river was swollen, and he said, "Not yet!" Because of this, people suspected he wasn't crazy.

3. Also called Zhao Wu; a minister of state during the Spring and Autumn era, noted as a social reformer.
4. In Shanxi.

Many of his statements proved true. Everyone thought he was a hermit. He died at the age of eighty-nine.

Taoist Silence

SHI DELIN

Shi Delin was a man of Anding.[5] In 210, when chaos reigned in the heartland,[6] he went south into Hanzhong.[7] He never pursued any profession and never married or fathered children. He constantly read the five-thousand-character text of Lao-tzu, as well as various esoteric books, reciting them ceaselessly day and night.

When he didn't have enough to eat, he'd do some begging, but he didn't take much when he begged. When people asked his name, he wouldn't say. People of the time called him the Pauper. It seems he was one of those totally devoted to mystic silence.

Taoist Character

ZUO CI

Zuo Ci was styled Yuanfang. He was a man of Lujiang.[8] In youth he learned the Five Classics and mastered astrology as well. Seeing the fortune of the Han dynasty about to end, with disorder arising throughout the land, he lamented, "In this time of decline, those in high offices are in danger, while those with a lot of property will die. Glory in the present age is not worth hankering after."

So he studied Taoist arts and meditated on Pillar of Heaven Mountain.[9] Finding an alchemical scripture in a cave, he put it into practice and could transform in myriad ways.

Cao Cao summoned him to test him, wishing to learn the Way from him. Ci said, "To learn the Way requires purity, without con-

---

5. In Gansu.
6. As the Han dynasty was finally dissolving, that is, and being dismembered by warlords into the Three Kingdoms.
7. In Shaanxi.
8. In Anhui.
9. In Anhui.

trivance; it is not suitable for those in high positions." Cao was envious by nature and repeatedly tried to kill him but was unable to do so.

When Ci was in Xing province, Liu Biao was governor; he too wanted to kill Ci, thinking him to be confusing the populace. Knowing of this beforehand, Ci went away from Biao, going east. Then when he met Sun Quan, the ruler of Wu, Quan already knew Ci had the Way, so he respected him courteously.

According to *Declarations of the Realized,* "Ci is now on Little Gua Mountain; always coming and going, he has repeatedly been down here seeking to take on more work. Ci's face appeared very young; he had indeed attained the benefits of the nine products of furnace and fire. He lives in seclusion in the Guacang Mountains.[10] Toward the end of the Jian-an era [196–220], Ci once crossed the river to visit Maoshan and got access to the caves. He also begged for cinnabar to compound nine-product elixir. He was a teacher of Li Zhongfu's disciple Ge Xuan."

GE XUAN

Ge Xuan was styled Xiaoxian. Learning the scriptural teachings from Zuo Yuanfang, he used to ingest atractylodes and was particularly advanced in the arts of healing and exorcism. He was able to reproduce his body and transform it.

The archruler of Wu insisted on meeting him. He wanted to confer a glorious rank on him, but Xuan wouldn't hear of it. He tried to leave but couldn't. He was treated courteously as a guest.

One day he said to his disciple Zhang Gong, "I am being constrained by the ruler of the realm to stay here, so I haven't had time to make the major medicine. Now I will depart in the middle of the thirteenth day of the eighth month."

When the designated time came, Xuan went into his room with his robe and hat on, lay down, and expired. The appearance of his face didn't change. His disciples burned incense and kept a vigil over him for three days and three nights.

In the middle of the third night, a tremendous wind arose, blowing open the room and snapping tree limbs, sounding like thunder, putting out the lamps. After quite a while they relit the lamps and found him gone. All they saw was his cast-off robe on the bed. The sash had not been untied.

10. In Jiangsu, tenth of the Ten Great Grotto Heavens of esoteric Taoism.

The next morning they questioned the neighbors, who said there had been no big wind. The wind was only in one house, but the fence and trees were both broken.

According to *Declarations of the Realized*, "Xuan was first on Changshan,[11] more recently went into Gaizhu.[12] He was able to ride tigers and command demons. There was nothing he didn't attain, but he ended up without having received a post."

The annotation of the Recluse [Tao Hongjing] says, "This was a paternal uncle of Baopu the Simpleton;[13] he was the teacher of Zhang Siyuan. When he was young he went into the mountains and attained immortality; at the time no one could find out where he was. It is related that an immortal in the Eastern Sea sent him a letter addressing him as an immortal, so the Simpleton likewise affirmed it."

BAO JING

Bao Jing was styled Taixuan. He was a man of Chenliu in Donghai. When he was five years old he said to his parents, "I was originally a child of the Li family in Quyang; when I was nine years old I fell into a well and died." His parents went and sought out the Li family; questioning them, they found that everything proved to be true.

Jing's studies included both the esoteric and the exoteric; he understood astronomy as well as the River and Luo writings. In public office he reached the rank of governor of Nanyang.

Once, on a tour of his jurisdiction, he went to sea. Blown away, he nearly starved. Then he gathered some white stones and boiled them, saving himself thereby.

Later he met the realized man Lord of Darkness, who transmitted secrets of the Way to him. He also studied with Zuo Yuanfang, from whom he received the middle-section teachings, the *Inner Writings of the Three August Ones*.[14] He was able to employ and compel ghosts

11. "Eternal Mountain," that is, Mount Heng.

12. Bamboo Cover Mountain in Zhejiang.

13. Ge Hong, self-styled Baopuzi, author of the famous book so named.

14. The account of Bao Jing in *Yunji qiqian* has "middle-section teachings, including the *Inner Writings of the Three August Ones*." There are a number of works classified in this category. Cf. *Daozang jiyao*, vol. 20, p. 8918. The earliest Three August Ones literature is attributed to Bo He, who studied with Lord Wang. The reputed provenience of Three August Ones resembles the much later Tibetan Buddhist *terton* tradition. For more by Ge Hong on this corpus, see the section "Xialan" of *Baopuzi*, in *Daozang jiyao*, vol. 11, p. 4892.

and spirits, seal mountains, and subjugate devils. He was more than a hundred years old when he died.

According to *Declarations of the Realized*, "Jing and his younger sister both reached their present degree of blessings due to the accumulated practices of secret charity by seven generations of ancestors. Now they are both lords of the underworld, inside Huayang."

The Recluse noted, "Jing used the Great Purity method of liberation from the corpse; he should be the highest type of lord. Jing's daughter, the Bao girl, was the wife of Ge Hong, the cavalier attendant in waiting."

Taoist Discourse

ZHANG XUANPIN

Zhang Xuanpin was a man of Dingxiang.[15] In the time of the Martial Lord of Wei[16] he was nominated for civil service examination in the category of *talented*. He returned to his native village and entered the tutelage of Master Su of West River, from whom he learned to ingest atractylodes preparations, and he also carried out the practice of the white element in the open room.[17] Later he met the realized man Fan Ziming on Few Houses Mountain, who transmitted to him the way of evasive transformation and concealment of appearance.

Formerly on Pillars of Heaven Mountain, later in Huayang, he was an earl in charge of prevention. The earls in charge of prevention are officers in charge of rain and water and also life-preserving supervisors of nations.

Xuanpin was good at discussing empty nothingness; he was an orator. He used to say, "Nothingness is the house of great being, which is why small being is born in it. Develop small being to nurture small nothingness; see great being to find the root of great nothingness.

15. In Shanxi.
16. That is, Cao Cao, who set himself up as king of Wei in 216 and was succeeded by his son in 220.
17. This refers to an inner visualization exercise in which a supernal being called the Lord of the White Element is visualized in the head. Cf. *Taishan dongfang neijing*, annotated at CH010349.

If you try to possess being, then there's nothing there; if you try to negate nothingness, then you affirm it. Therefore my eyes do not see anything at all, yet things do not appear nonexistent. Nothingness comes about based on being; nothingness is attained by means of nothing. With this, nothingness is the abode of nothing, and cosmic space houses nothingness. Before I was born, no one in the world had nothingness."

He said of himself, "I once went to Penglai,[18] where I discussed nothingness with Song Chensheng, Duke of the Left. I got a rough sense of the man's meaning; even the realized people on Pawlonia and Cedar Mountain couldn't refute it. Since then, I couldn't even take being as a basis; how could I take nothingness for a basis?" This is how high-minded and tenaciously logical he was.

Taoist Scholarship

WANG BI

Wang Bi was styled Fusi. He was a man of Gaoping in Shanyang.[19] When he was young he was perceptive and intelligent; he was already fond of Lao and Chuang when he was hardly more than ten years old. The secretary of the Ministry of Personnel, He Yan,[20] considered him very extraordinary; he said, "With someone like this, you can discuss the interaction of the divine and the human."

When Yan's own commentary on Lao-tzu was first completed, he went to Bi; seeing that Bi's commentary was exceptionally refined, Yan called his own commentary *Two Discourses on the Way and Virtue*. Yan also organized the best reasoning of predecessors and said to Bi, "This I consider ultimate—can you still criticize it?" Bi then made a critique, whereat everyone in attendance was confounded.

Bi used to maintain that the universe and all things have nothingness as a basis. Nothingness awakens people so they accomplish their work; wherever you go, it is there. Yin and yang depend on it to evolve

18. One of the fabled isles of the immortals.
19. In Shandong.
20. He Yan (d. 249) was also a great scholar and commentator, associated with the so-called *qingtan*, or pure conversation, fashion.

and produce, myriad things depend on it to materialize concretely; the wise depend on it to develop character, the unworthy depend on it for personal escape. So it has no rank yet is noble.

Bi wrote a commentary on the *I Ching*, which was followed by Confucians of yore.

[6]

JIN DYNASTY
(265–420)

Taoist Silence

SUN DENG

Sun Deng was styled Gonghe. He was a man of Jijun.[1] He had no home or family; he lived in a hole in the ground he made in the mountains north of the district. He liked reading the *I Ching*, and he played a one-string lute.

He never got angry, by nature. When some people threw him into water to see him get mad, he came out of the water laughing.

Once when he was staying in the mountains of Yiyang,[2] a charcoal maker saw him and knew he was not an ordinary man. He spoke to him, but Deng did not reply.

Emperor Wen [of Wei, r. 220–227] heard of him and sent Ruan Ji to go see him. When he found Deng he spoke to him, but Deng didn't answer him either.

Ji Kang followed Deng in his wanderings for three years, asking what he was aiming for, but he never answered. As Kang was about to leave, he said, "Have you nothing to say, after all?" Deng then said, "Do you know fire? When it comes into being it has light, but it does not use its light, though its effectiveness is in the use of light. People are born with abilities, but they don't use their abilities, though effectiveness is in the use of abilities. So to use light is a matter of obtaining firewood, so as to keep up its glow; the use of abilities is a matter of discerning reality, in order to complete your life. Now, you have lots of ability but little discernment—it'll be hard for you to be free from the present world. Have you nothing to seek?"

1. In Henan.
2. In Henan.

Kang couldn't make use of this. Later he wrote in a poem entitled "Hidden Resentments": "In the past I was embarrassed by Liuxia; now I'm shamed by Sun Deng."

No one knows where Sun Deng ended up.

Taoist Disposition[3]

GUO WEN

Guo Wen was styled Wenju. He was a man of Zhi east of the Yellow River.[4] When he was young he loved the mountains and rivers and valued escape. Whenever he'd go roaming in the mountains, he'd forget to return for ten days at a time.

When his parents finally completed his initiation into adulthood, he didn't marry; he left home and traveled to famous mountains. He always wore deer hide and a turban of arrowroot cloth. He gathered bamboo leaves and tree fruits and traded salt to support himself. When he had leftover grain from his meals, he'd donate it to the indigent.

Wang Dao[5] heard of him and sent someone to invite him. When he arrived, he was lodged in the west gardens.

Wen Jiao[6] once asked him, "How come you have no feelings?"

Guo Wen said, "Feelings come from thinking. I don't think, so I have no feelings."

Jiao also asked, "You stay alone in inaccessible mountains; if you get sick and die, you may be eaten by birds. Don't you regard that as miserable?"

Wen said, "Those who are buried in the ground get eaten by ants— what's the difference?"

Wang Dao once got a lot of guests together, with strings and woodwinds playing in concert. As a test he had Guo Wen called. Wen's gaze never shifted; he strode into the magnificently decorated hall as if he were walking in the woods and wilds.

All the guests in attendance at the time had sayings that fished out

3. The word used for *disposition* here means "substance" and implies inborn nature or character.
4. In Henan.
5. Wang Dao was a minister of state for Emperor Yuan of the Jin dynasty (r. 317–323) and mentor to his successors Emperor Ming (r. 323–325) and Emperor Cheng (r. 326–342).
6. Wen Jiao was a famous military and civil officer of the Jin dynasty, particularly noted for his role in quelling the rebellion of Su Jun mentioned below.

the profound and savored the remote, but Wen was always able to match anything said to him. His natural intelligence was immense; no one could peer through its door.

One day he suddenly sought leave to return to the mountains. Then when Su Jun[7] rebelled, everyone took it that he had recognized the subtle indications.

After he died, Ge Hong and Yu Zhan[8] both wrote stories eulogizing his virtues. In the Jianhua era [911–914] of the Liang dynasty he was entitled Spiritually Radiant Lord of the Real.

Ji Kang

Ji Kang was styled Shuye. He was a man of Zhi prefecture in the state of Qiao.[9] He was orphaned early. He had extraordinary talent, far beyond the crowd. He was more than six feet three inches tall.[10] He was eloquent and handsome, but he made his appearance plain and didn't dress up. People considered him distinguished and elegant, but it was innate, naturally so.

He studied without instruction from teachers, read widely and comprehended everything. He was married into the ruling family of Wei and was given a prestige title. He used to practice nurturing nature and ingesting elixirs. He played the lute and sang poetry, enough to comfort his heart.

He considered spiritual immortality to be an endowment from nature, not a product of learning. As for reasonable exercise and nutrition, the standards of Anqi[11] and Grandfather Peng[12] could be reached, so he wrote *Discourse on Nurturing Life*.

7. Su Jun (d. 328) was a military and civil leader under the Jin dynasty who rebelled and usurped the power of the throne but then was ultimately overthrown.
8. A distinguished civil servant under the Jin dynasty, holding the posts of minister of works, palace steward, and provincial governor.
9. In Anhui.
10. Seven *chi* eight *cun*: based on these measures as of Jin times, this would be somewhat more than six feet three inches. Presumably this was above average for his time and place.
11. Anqi Sheng is a legendary immortal associated with the island of Penglai. He is supposed to have lived more than a thousand years. The First Emperor of China, who was intensely interested in immortality, is said to have met Anqi on a journey east.
12. Grandfather Peng is supposed to have lived for eight hundred years. A manual on energy-induction exercises attributed to him can be found in the *Baopuzi*. See *Daozang jiyao*, vol. 20, p. 8686.

Those with whom he always considered spiritual communication genuine were only Ruan Ji of Chenliu and Shan Tao of Henei, while those who joined their set were Xiang Xiu, Liu Ling, Ji's nephew Han, and Wang Ru, eventually making up the Bamboo Grove association.

Ru said he'd lived with Kang in Shenyang for twenty years and never once saw him either angry or joyful.

Kang used to gather herbs, roaming mountains and wetlands. When he'd get into a good mood, he'd become ecstatic and forget to return. The occasional woodcutter or thatch cutter who encountered him thought he was a spirit man.

He went to the mountains of Ji county,[13] where he saw Sun Deng and then went wandering along with him. Deng was sunk in silence and self-contained; he didn't talk or say anything. When Kang was about to leave, he asked for a word of advice. Deng said, "Your talent is of a high order, but your way of preserving your body is inadequate."

He also met Wang Lie, and they went into the mountains together. Lie once found some stone marrow like rock sugar. He ingested half and gave the rest to Kang. In both cases it crystallized.

Wang also once saw a silk text in a cavern and immediately called Kang to go get it, but suddenly it could no longer be seen. Lie lamented, "Shuye's mentality is extraordinary, and yet even though he looked right away he couldn't find it. That's fate."

When Shan Tao was about to leave, he was selected for office but recommended Kang in his stead. Kang then presented Shan Tao with a letter announcing termination of contact. In sum it said, "I have heard the sayings left by Taoists, that ingesting polygonatum and atractylodes enables people to prolong the life span, and I have a lot of confidence in this. Roaming the mountains and wilds, watching birds and fish, is a pleasure to my heart. Were I to become an official, I'd have to give all of this up. How can I abandon what I enjoy to pursue what I fear! Now I just want to stay in a humble neighborhood, raise my children and grandchildren, from time to time express my feelings about separation and distance from relatives and friends, talking about the old days. A cup of unfiltered wine, a tune on the lute— that's the extent of my ambition!"

Now that this had been put in writing, it was obvious he couldn't be compelled or constrained.

13. In Henan.

The governor of Nanhai, Bao Jing, was one in communion with the miraculous; Xu Ning of Donghai took him for his teacher. One night Ning heard the sound of a lute in Jing's room; marveling at its refinement, he asked about it. Jing said, "That was Ji Shuye." Ning said, "Ji was killed—how could he be here?"[14]

Jing said, "Shuye projected the appearance of dying, but in reality he just left the body."

This appears in Gu Kaizhi's[15] eulogy of Ji Kang.

RUAN JI

Ruan Ji was styled Sizong. He was a man of Yushi in Chenliu.[16] His appearance was well proportioned and distinguished, his temperament was broad-minded and free. Haughty and self-satisfied, he did as he pleased, without constraint, yet neither joy nor anger ever showed on his face.

Sometimes he'd shut himself indoors and read books for months on end. Sometimes he'd climb mountains and gaze upon rivers, forgetting to come back for days at a stretch.

He was widely read but was particularly fond of Chuang-tzu and Lao-tzu. He once wrote *A Discourse on Understanding Chuang-tzu*,

---

14. The Ming dynasty scholar Li Zhi recounts the story of Ji Kang's murder in his *Zangshu:*

"Kang was poor and supported himself by working as a smith. In those days Zhong Hui, a friend of Sima Zhao, heard of Kang and went to visit him. Hui was a distinguished gentleman, esteemed for talent and ability, who rode on hefty horses and wore lightweight clothes, with a huge crowd of hangers-on. Kang kept working at his forge and didn't pay attention. Hui was impressed with him.

"When Shan Tao was chosen to be a courtier, he nominated Kang instead. Kang wrote a letter refusing and cutting off contact, explaining that he personally could not stand current customs, not that he was slighting the example of sagacious kings of old. So when Sima Zhao heard of this, he hated Kang.

"Kang was on good terms with Lu Zhao and his younger brother An. An was smitten with Kang's loftiness and would go to any lengths for him. Now, Lu Zhao had an illicit affair with An's wife and then condemned An for disrespect and had him imprisoned. An called on Kang to testify for him. Kang's sense of justice was not without appreciation, so he explained the matter.

"Like Kang, An was also very zealous in his will to save the world. Zhong Hui urged Lu Zhao to take this opportunity to get rid of him. So he killed An, and Kang too."

15. Gu Kaizhi (345–406) was a poet, painter, and courtier.

16. In Henan.

setting forth the value of not being artificial, but it is lengthy so I won't cite it. He composed more than eight thousand (or, according to the *Book of Jin,* eighty) verses, *Poems Expressing Thoughts,* which were esteemed by the world. He enjoyed wine, was an able whistler, and was good at playing the lute. When he was satisfied, he'd forget himself, and many people of the time thought him an imbecile.

When he heard that the quartermaster of the infantry was a good brewer and had a store of three hundred casks of wine, Ruan Ji sought to be made commander of the infantry and set aside worldly affairs.

He was also able to show favor or contempt in his eyes. When he'd see gentlemen who were ritual conventionalists, he'd look upon them with contempt.

Once he met Sun Deng in the Sumen Mountains[17] and tried to discuss eternity and the arts of calming the mind and energizing the body, but Deng didn't reply to anything. Ji therefore left, whistling all the way. When he got to the middle of the mountain ridge, he heard a sound like the song of a phoenix echoing through the canyon; it was Sun Deng whistling.

When he got home, he wrote *The Story of a Great Man.* In sum it said, "What the world calls a lordly man only learns the law and only masters courtesy; his hands hold ceremonial jade, his feet walk a straight line. In his actions he wishes to be an example for the time; in his words he wishes to be a standard for eternity. When young he is praised in his hometown, as an adult he is known in the neighboring states. He would aim for the highest offices above while not disregarding regional governance below. Only he doesn't see lice in his underwear, hiding in the inner seams, concealed in frayed lining, taking these to be auspicious abodes. When they creep they dare not leave the borders of the seams, when they squirm they dare not leave the underwear—and they think they're conforming to standards and rules. Then let the hills ignite and the fire flow, burning towns and destroying cities; the lice will stay in the underpants, unable to get out. How is a lordly man living in a city different from this?"

This was also Ji's basic inclination. He used to ride alone at will, not going by the roads. When his chariot got stuck and couldn't go any farther, he'd cry out in lament and turn back.

17. In Henan.

Once he climbed Guangwu Mountain[18] to gaze on the battleground of Han and Chu. He lamented, "When an era lacks heroes, it lets punks become famous."

He died in 263.

Taoist Scholars

XIANG XIU

Xiang Xiu was styled Ziqi. He was a man of Huai east of the Yellow River.[19] Clear in understanding, he had far-reaching perception and was fond of studying Lao-tzu and Chuang-tzu. He was recognized by Shan Tao in his youth.

Xiu interpreted the inner and outer chapters of *Chuang-tzu* beyond the old annotations, subtly teasing out extraordinary points, greatly expounding mysticism. Only two chapters, "Autumn Waters" and "Ultimate Happiness," remained unfinished. In the time of Emperor Hui (r. 290–307), Guo Xiang[20] expanded upon this commentary.

Xiu was friends with Ji Kang and Lu An, but their inclinations were not the same. Kang looked down on the world and was unconstrained, An was self-indulgent and unconventional, while Xiu was devoted to reading. When Xiu was going to write his commentary on Chuang-tzu, he first told Kang and An. They both said, "Why does this book need any further comment? You'd just be discarding others' work and pursuing a hobby." But then when it was done, he showed it to the two, saying, "Would you still insist on stopping me?" Surprised, Kang and An said, "Chuang-tzu hasn't died!"

He also commented on the *I Ching*. For overall meaning it is worth reading, but it compares with the Confucians of the Han dynasty and is not peerless like *The Hidden Chuang*, his commentary on *Chuang-tzu*.

Kang was also a good smith, and Xiu used to assist him. They'd work together merrily, oblivious to all else.

18. In Henan.
19. In Henan.
20. Guo Xiang's commentary on the *Chuang-tzu* is generally accorded highest prestige. A traditional encomium quips that it is not clear whether Guo Xiang is commenting on Chuang-tzu or Chuang-tzu is commenting on Guo Xiang.

Later he went to Luoyang in response to the accounts assistant of his home county. Emperor Wen asked him, "I hear you have the aspiration to retire to the mountains; what are you doing here?" Xiu said, "It's because purists like Chao and Xu[21] didn't understand Yao's[22] heart. How are they worthy of much admiration?" The emperor was delighted.

After that, when a neighbor was playing the flute, the notes were so clear that Xiu was reminded of his past friendship and association with Ji Kang and wrote *Nostalgic Elegy*. He had reached the rank of cavalier attendant in waiting when he died.

HUANGFU MI

Huangfu Mi was styled Shi-an. As a child he was named Jing. He was a man of Anding.[23] He was a great-grandson of Defender in Chief Song of the Han dynasty.

At the age of twenty he was disinclined to study, but later in life he studied books with a man from his village, Xi Tan. Living in poverty, he carried classic texts with him as he plowed, eventually mastering the classic books and the sayings of the philosophers. Plunging into quietude and minimizing desire, he began to have lofty aspirations and made writing his occupation. Calling himself Professor of Mystic Repose, he wrote treatises on manners and music, rulers and real people.

Later on he was afflicted with rheumatism, but he was never without a book in hand. When people urged him to cultivate his reputation and broaden his contacts, he responded by writing *A Treatise on Preserving the Profound*: "Poverty is the norm for a gentleman, lowliness is the reality of the Way." So he didn't serve in government after all.

Absorbed in the classics, he forgot about his ailment and neglected to eat. Contemporaries called him a book addict. When someone admonished his excessive earnestness, warning he'd wear out his vital spirit, Mi said, "'If one hears the Way in the morning, it is all right if

21. Chao Fu and Xu You, whom legend has disdaining the throne in ancient times. See above, notes to the story of Jiao Zhen.
22. The model sage king Yao, who is said to have ceded the throne on the basis of merit rather than hereditary succession.
23. In Gansu.

he dies that night!'[24] Moreover, the length of one's allotted life span depends on heaven."

He was recommended in the category of *filial and honest* for the post of senior counselor in chief and also recommended for examination in the category of *chief of the wise and good*, but he didn't respond at all. Yet when he wrote personally to Emperor Wu [of Jin] to borrow texts, the emperor sent him a whole cartload of books.

In spite of his affliction, he read tirelessly. Although repeatedly summoned, he never served in government. He died in 281. The collections of stories he wrote, such as *Genealogies of Emperors and Kings*, *Eminent Gentlemen*, *Free Men*, and *Chaste Women*, were all respected in the world.

Taoist Character

GE HONG

Ge Hong was styled Zhichuan. He was a man of Jurong in Danyang.[25] He took a liking to study when he was young, but his family was poor, so he cut firewood by himself to sell for paper and ink. At night he'd copy books, study and recite, eventually becoming known for scholarship.

By nature he had few desires, and he had no hobbies. He didn't even know how to play chess or dice games. His personality was plain, and he had no interest in fame or fortune. He closed his door, kept people away, and never socialized. Sometimes, however, to search out a book or inquire into a principle, he wouldn't consider a thousand miles far; he'd venture over steep mountain paths, determined to obtain what he sought. He was particularly fond of the doctrines of spiritual immortality and physical culture. His uncle Xuan studied the Way and attained immortality in Wu times; he was called Immortal Master Ge. He passed on his secret arts of alchemy to his disciple Zheng Yin; Hong studied from Yin and acquired the whole science.

In the 320s the minister of education Wang Dao summoned him to assist the county recorder. Later he was selected to be senior recorder

---

24. This quote is a famous saying by Confucius.
25. In Jiangsu.

in charge of important drafts, but he stoutly refused to take up these positions.

Later in life he wanted to cook up alchemical elixir, and hearing that Jiaozhi[26] produced cinnabar, sought to be made governor of Goulu. The emperor thought he had a high potential and didn't permit this. Hong said, "It's not for glory but just because there's cinnabar there." The emperor agreed to this.

On the way, when he came to Guangzhou, the regional inspector, Deng Yue, tried to get him to stay there, but he wouldn't agree and left. Then he stayed on Mount Luofu,[27] where he cooked elixir. He spent years on the mountain, roaming freely and leisurely taking care of his health while writing unceasingly.

His own introduction says: "I am personally lacking in the ability to try to get ahead; I happen to like the occupation of not striving. Even if I could fly up to the sky by flapping my wings, even if I could chase the wind and run after the sunlight by making my legs gallop, I'd still rather fold my sturdy wings in a flock of little quail and hide my fleet tracks in the company of lame donkeys.

"How much the more so since earth has given me ordinary short wings, Creation has lent me extremely slow, lame legs. Those who figure themselves out are clear; those who cannot do so get stymied. How dare I try to force a housefly to soar through the heavens or whip a lame nag to pursue the course of the moon? This is why I've given up any hope of a glorious career and aimed for peace in a realm of destitution.

"Wild spinach and beans are as delicious as delicacies; a hovel is as comfortable as a mansion. Secular scholars only know obedience to the Duke of Zhou and Confucius; none of them believe in the books of spiritual immortals. Not only do they laugh at them, they thereby repudiate truth. So the book I've written, in 116 inner and outer chap-

26. This refers to Tonkin, the heartland of what is now the northern part of Vietnam, which was under Chinese control from the late second century B.C.E. to the early tenth century C.E. The name Jiaozhi means "entrepôt," and this was an important link between southern and northern Asia. It was a commercial and administrative hub of Guangzhou, which at that time included Guangdong and Guangxi. Goulu, where Ge Hong sought a post for access to cinnabar, was in Guángxi. The name is now used to refer to a dialect.

27. In Guangdong, seventh of the Ten Great Grotto Heavens of Taoism.

ters, *The Simpleton,* may be unworthy of deposit on a famous mountain, but I want to seal it in a gold box to show to connoisseurs."

It seems he named the book after his own epithet, Baopuzi, He Who Embraces Simplicity. Hong's vast learning was unmatched left of the River,[28] and the volume of his writings exceeded that of Ban Gu and Sima Qian.[29] Also, he clearly elucidated the abstruse, analyzing principles subtly.

One day he sat till noon, then died without moving, as if he'd fallen asleep. He was eighty-one years old. His face appeared as if alive, and his body was flexible. When they lifted him into the casket, he was as light as empty clothing. It seems he had been liberated from the corpse and become immortal.

Taoism and Authority

WANG XIZHI

Wang Xizhi was styled Yishao. He was a nephew of Minister of Education Wang Dao. He was skilled at calligraphy in the clerical script, considered the best in history. Critics said that his brushstrokes were as buoyant as drifting clouds yet as powerful as startled dragons. He used to say of himself, "My calligraphy, compared with Zhong Yao's,[30] is on a par; compared with Zhang Zhi's[31] cursive calligraphy, it is like a younger to an elder brother."

He was deeply respected by his uncle for his potential. Starting out as a clan secretary, later he became general of the Right Army, chamberlain for Huiji.

Xizhi liked to take medicines and nurture nature; he didn't enjoy being in the capital city. When he first crossed over to Zhejiang, he immediately resolved to stay there for the rest of his life. Huiji has beautiful mountains and rivers, and a lot of famous gentlemen lived

28. South of the Yangzi River. An exodus of Jin aristocracy from the north had taken place around 311 when Huns sacked Luoyang and captured the Chinese emperor.

29. Ban Gu (32–92) and Sima Qian (ca. 145–90 B.C.E.) were classical historians whose works set the precedents for the two dominant models of traditional Chinese historiography.

30. Zhong Yao (151–230) was a distinguished calligrapher of the Han dynasty.

31. Zhang Zhi (d. 192 C.E.) is credited with developing the modern cursive style.

there. Xie An[32] also lived there before he entered government service. Once he held a gathering of colleagues at a resort in Shanyin; Xizhi himself wrote the introduction. When someone compared it to Fan Yue's[33] *Gold Valley Poems* preface, Wang Xizhi was likened to Shi Chong,[34] which pleased him very much when he heard it.

He had a natural fondness for geese. There was a Taoist in Shanyin who raised five geese, and Xizhi went to see them. He was delighted and wanted to buy one. The Taoist said, "If you'll write a copy of the *Tao Te Ching* for me, I'll give you the whole gaggle." Xizhi happily copied out the whole text and came back with a cage of geese. That's how spontaneous he was.

Later he went back to his hometown, claiming to be ill, and wrote a document before his parents' graves pledging that he would never again go into government service. Once he had left office, he wandered all over mountains and rivers with people of the East. He also practiced ingesting elixirs and gathering medicines with the maestro Xu Mai. He was fifty-nine when he died.

Taoist Character

Xu Mai

Xu Mai was styled Shuxuan. One of his names was Ying. He was a man of Jurong in Danyang. He was fond of the Way from boyhood, secretly attaining mystic experiences. Once he was divining under the guidance of Guo Pu[35] and came upon the top yin line of the hexagram Great Power [another version says it was the top yin of Tran-

---

32. Xie An (320–385) was a famous statesman of the Jin dynasty.

33. A civil servant, courtier, and writer of the Jin dynasty. He was very famous for his literary talent and had many female admirers, but he was ultimately executed through an intrigue stemming from factional rivalry.

34. Shi Chong was noted for brilliance from youth and entered government service in his teens. He retired and went to sea in his late twenties, became wealthy and married a beautiful woman, then became notorious for flaunting his wealth in competition with others, and was finally framed by a man who coveted his wife. It is not quite clear why Wang Xizhi would have been pleased to be compared to Shi Chong, except perhaps in respect to his legendary brilliance and early success.

35. Guo Pu (276–324) was a natural historian associated with the development of feng shui.

quillity].[36] When what the line revealed became clear, Guo Pu told him, "Your great fortune is from heaven; you should study the path of ascension."

At first he took Bao Jing as his teacher and received the middle-section teachings, including the *Inner Writings of the Three August Ones*. One day he left home. Considering that Mount Xianliu in Yuhang is near Maoshan in Yanling and, being on the eastern portal of Dongting, had secret routes to the Five Mountains, which Chen Anshi[37] and Mao Jiwei[38] had traveled, he built a cloister on Xianliu and went back and forth to the Maoshan caves. At the times of the new moon and the full moon alone he'd go back home to look in on his family. Once his parents had died, he sent his wife back to her family, let his hair down, and left all cares behind. He changed his name to Xuan, and his style to Yuanyou.

Through Xu Mai's dealings with General of the Right Army Wang and son, Wang took to practicing respect for his father, teachers, and ruler. Xu Mai once sent Wang a letter saying, "From Shanyin south to Lin-an there are a lot of sanctuaries, immortals, and sacred mushrooms; disciples of Zuo Yuanfang, those who attained the Way as the Han dynasty ended, are all there."

In the autumn of 348 he disappeared into the mountains west of Linan. Then he went to stay on Red Mountain in Linhai.[39] He met good friends Wang Shilong, Zhao Daoxuan, and Fu Taichu. Subsequently he took Shilong as his teacher and was taught the way to release and practiced the reverse movement method.[40] Ingesting jade

36. Great Power is symbol 34 in the *I Ching*. Tranquillity is symbol 11. In both symbols the top line is yin, or negative; in Great Power it is associated with an exhortation to overcome obstacles when at an impasse; in Tranquillity it is associated with a warning to take timely measures to preserve tranquillity before it is too late to prevent its loss.

37. Chen Anshi was an immortal of the latter Han dynasty. He was a menial in the house of a man who was interested in immortalism, and his potential was recognized by sages his employer had invited. Eventually his employer became his disciple. Chen is one of those who is supposed to have ascended to heaven in broad daylight. An account of him appears in Ge Hong's *Legends of Spiritual Immortals*.

38. Mao Jiwei was the middle Mao brother.

39. In Zhejiang.

40. This is described in *Yunji qiqian*; cf. *Daozang jiyao*, vol. 19, p. 8583a.

juice,[41] courting brain vitality,[42] within two or three years his face had a glow. Having rejuvenated his face, he finally thought he'd attained the Way.

At this point Director of Destiny Mao commanded the lord of permanent records to recommend him, having a report made to the Upper Palace, transferring his name to the east, and registering him as an earthly immortal.[43]

Now the chief security chamberlain for the Three Offices[44] sent the lord in charge of authority, Zhou Fang, and the agent in charge of wrongdoers, Yan Baihu, to come to Red Mountain in order to arrest Xu Mai and remove him. They questioned him about his indictment, moreover, producing records of sin on cinnabar slips, each holding a statement and interrogating him: "Those who wish to study the Way in hopes of life follow the realized people above, to deepen their minds to reside in the remote and to be reverently truthful to the spiritually elevated, should have corresponding accomplishments in the world, so calamity and evil do not occur, hidden charity flows from the roots, and human hearts reach up above. Only then can you walk toward truth and seek immortality, passing on your name to the cave government. What about the fact that your father personally killed Xie Gong and rebelled against the sun, moon, and stars? Also, Xu Chao had Li Fan's head cut off instead of decapitating Cai Fu, dis-

41. This generally refers to swallowing saliva, a common practice in Taoist health-maintenance regimes.
42. This refers to the practice of mentally conducting vital energy up the spine into the brain. See *Essential Secrets for Visualization According to the Immortals' Ancient Books of Great Clarity* in *Vitality, Energy, Spirit* (Thomas Cleary, 1991), pp. 148–50; *Some Questions on Alchemy* in *The Book of Balance and Harmony* (Thomas Cleary, 1986), pp. 52–58; and *Spiritual Alchemy for Women* in *Immortal Sisters* (Thomas Cleary, 1989), pp. 94–99.
43. These offices pertain to the esoteric organization of the Maoshan cult; see the end of this story.
44. These offices are a construct of the Celestial Masters cult descended from Zhang Daoling. The Three Offices of sky, earth, and water were said to record the misdeeds of humans. This story, found in *Declarations of the Realized,* appears to represent a jurisdictional dispute between the Maoshan cult and the Celestial Masters cult. Eventually these major movements and certain other mountain-based sects of southern China would merge portions of their respective authority in the True Unity denomination of Taoism.

missed and executed Pan Qi and others, dismembered the commander Cao Bian and others, sank Tang Yun's corpse in water, incinerated
Xu Geng's body, strangled Huan Ang to death, and eviscerated Zhen
Kuai. His unjust executions numbered forty-three, on trumped-up
false charges. The case is before the Celestial Lord. With malignant
perversities piled high as a mountain, he accomplished nothing good
at all.

"Also, you and your father originally belonged to the Bo Family
Way,[45] sacrificing animals for the benefit of people; unrequited wrongs
and accumulated blame are listed in the Three Offices, yet you've been
exceptionally lucky to escape the law and follow the energy of reality.
Father and son, each serves a master and has similarly committed offenses, not collaborating with the Elders;[46] the magnitude of your
wrongdoings is about to be subjected to an occult investigation. With
such accumulated misdeeds, and given the fact that no immortal can
fool an officer of the Supreme, can you be allowed to have your name
inscribed in the purple register of the undying? If you have no reply, the
officers will arrest you."

Ying [Xu Mai] stood firm, whistling all the while, brushing off his
coarse wool clothing and patting down his hair. Then he got serious
and spoke out in a loud, accusatory voice: "The Great Way has no
relatives; only goodness is its associate. Heaven and earth are im-
personal; they show compassion according to virtue. Therefore the

45. This was a cult of Wei and Jin times ultimately absorbed into the Maoshan and
Celestial Masters cults. The surname Bo was common among sinicized Kuchans, a
central Asian people, and it may be that the particulars of animal sacrifice to which
objection appears to be made here (and in more detail in *Declarations of the Realized*) derived from practices of non-Chinese origin. Animal sacrifice in itself was not
alien to ancient Chinese culture, but it was increasingly disfavored by Confucian hu-
manitarians and was anathema to Buddhism, which was spreading in China at this
time. A number of prominent Buddhists of central Asian origin or ancestry working
in China, including the famous magician Fotuteng (who appears in a supporting role
later in this work) had the surname Bo. Taoist records list at least two masters with
this name, but their connection with this cult, and other details of the movement,
are obscure.

46. This is a term used in the Celestial Master cult for a community leader. In secular terminology it literally means "toastmaster" and refers to the elder or senior
scholar at a gathering of learned men.

Yellow Emperor spilled blood at Banquan[47] without its disqualifying him for ascent on a dragon; the Three Miao stained the fields scarlet, reddening the grasses at Zhuolu,[48] but did that interfere with the spiritual influence of the great sage, or lofty understanding and superior attainment?

"My paternal forefather Xu Zi'a, seventh generation before me, had long-established habits of humaneness and distinguished virtue, secretly aiding even birds and beasts. In bad years when the people were starving and epidemics raged, affecting 99 percent of the population, he would distribute his private resources to help out the common folk, personally preparing prescriptions and medicines, so diligent in his labors that he would lodge away from home. When someone died, he was as if he'd lost a parent; he saved other people from affliction as if it were his own illness. When the doomed were in Zi'a's hands, he treated their nearly exhausted bodies like his own children, getting them through bad years; those people who survived because of Zi'a numbered 408. His humanity and charity were unfailing and subsequently should be concentrated in us. So his record of merit has gone up to the Supreme Deity, his virtue has been published in the spiritual palace, causing my ancestral roots to spread and my clan to flourish, protecting and enlightening descendants, thus causing branches to grow to flower and bloom. Born with an inclination for immortality, there have been five people qualified to transcend the world and three people who ascended. Their names are recorded with

47. This is a signal event in legendary history, alleged to have taken place in the twenty-sixth century B.C.E. The Yellow Emperor, a central cultural and tribal ancestor of the Chinese people, led a coalition of tribes against the people of the Red Emperor, who were overcome and integrated. The Red Emperor stands for Shennong, the Agricultural Genius or Spirit Farmer, who thus came to be considered an earlier ancestor of the Chinese people.

48. The Three Miao were one of the most populous and powerful rivals of the people of the Yellow Emperor, prehistoric ancestors of the Chinese. *Zhuolu* refers to the second major war in Chinese history, in which the Yellow Emperor, now allied with the tribe of the Red Emperor, overcame an alliance of peoples including the Three Miao and the Jiuli tribes. The attacks of the Jiuli on the Red Emperor's tribe had originally driven it into territorial conflict with the Yellow Emperor's tribe, and the Yellow-Red alliance that emerged from the battle of Banquan then turned on the Jiuli and their Miao allies. The wars of exalted ancestors are conventionally cited to counter the Confucian stigma on warfare and punishment, by inferring that benevolence may sometimes require violence.

the Supreme, on slips in the Green Palace. How could your ilk appreciate that?"

When he'd finished speaking, Fang and Baihu burst out laughing. At that time the lord in charge of destiny sent the scout Li Zun, who came with a bell in hand to summon him and take him in. At this point Fang and Baihu simply ran away.

Before Li Zun came, Ying had been scared out of his wits. He also relied on his teacher Wang Shilong for help. When Ying made his answer, he still nearly failed. Now he was enabled to deliver his name to the Eastern Palace, to become a midlevel immortal.[49]

In 913 he was entitled Lord of the Real, Restored to Unity.

The lord in charge of destiny was the elder master Mao.

Taoism and Authority

XIE AN

Xie An was styled Anshi. He was a man of Yangxia in Chun prefecture.[50] A hereditary scholar, he was already famous for learning and conduct when he was young. Lodging in Huiji, when he went out it was to go hunting and fishing in the mountains and rivers; when he stayed in he'd read and write. He had no worldly ambitions. Sitting in a stone chamber overlooking a deep valley, he sighed pensively and said, "How far even Bo Yi is from here!"

An was good at talking about *Chuang-tzu* and *Lao-tzu*. One day he got together with Zhi [Daolin][51] and Xu [Mai] at Wang Meng's house.

---

49. This pertains to the esoteric hierarchy of the Maoshan cult.

50. In Henan.

51. Zhi Daolin (Zhi Dun, 314–366) was a famous Buddhist. While he was from a Buddhist family, he was not ordained as a monk until he was twenty-five years old, and he maintained contacts among the intellectual elite of his time. The name Zhi comes from Yuezhi, the Chinese name of a central Asian people with whom China had important cultural contacts. According to *Biographies of Eminent Monks I* (4), Zhi's original surname was Guan, which one line of explanation attributes to descendants of Officer Xi, Keeper of the Pass (Guan), the subject of the first story in this collection. Since the pass that Xi manned was between China and central Asia, there is no particular problem presuming connection between his posterity and people of Yuezhi. Zhi Dun is said to have come from Henan or Hedong and may have come from a lineage of Guoshi, "Attendants of the Nation," sons of nobles from central Asia educated in China.

An said to the others, "Today may be called a meeting of gentlemen. Since time cannot be stopped, this gathering certainly cannot last. Let's all recite poetry to reveal our thoughts."

Xu then asked the host if he had a copy of *Chuang-tzu*. He just found the chapter "The Fisherman." Xie looked at the title, then invited everyone to express themselves. Zhi Daolin went first, composing about seven hundred words, finely and beautifully set forth, with extraordinary ability and artistry, praised by the whole group.

Then each of them expressed his thoughts. Finally An asked, "Are you all finished?" They all said, "What's been said today is too little to be exhaustive on its own." An followed up with some general criticism, then set forth his own ideas, composing more than ten thousand words, the peak of his talent standing out. Unable to restrain himself, becoming even more animated, he went on making metaphors, annoyingly self-satisfied, tiresome to all.

Zhi Daolin said to him, "You run on obsessively, so after all you're just admiring yourself."

At that time the [future] emperor Jianwen [r. 371–373] was a prime minister. He said, "Since Anshi shares people's happiness, he cannot but share their grief as well. If I summon him he is sure to come."

In those days, his younger brother Wan was in charge of the responsibilities for the royal domains, an important position; yet though An was in the imperial guard, his repute was equal to Wan's, so it was naturally hoped he'd go into civil service. He was more than forty years old before he had an ambition to advance in office.

The chief general of campaigns against the nations to the west asked him to be a commander. As he was about to set out from Xinding,[52] the knights of the court all saw him off. Gao Song teased him, "You've repeatedly disregarded the command of the court, remaining aloof in the eastern mountains. Whenever anyone talks to you, you refuse to come forth. What can you do for the people? And now what can the people do for you?"

An later became prime minister. He found there was a lot of plotting in the ruling house of Jin, yet he was able to keep people under control by superior calculation. While talking and laughing at ease, he

---

52. In Jiangsu.

broke Huan Wen's[53] unruly temper; employing people of talent, he defeated Fu Jian's[54] million-man army. His accomplishments were in no way inferior to those of Wang Dao or Wen Jiao.[55]

Although An was relied upon by the court, his will to retire from the world never changed. When he went to occupy New City, his whole family made preparations to go to sea; he wanted the administration of the central government to be generally stable, then he'd return east from the river region. He died before his noble aim had been achieved.

By imperial decree he was given the posthumous office of mentor and the posthumous name Wenjing, Cultured Peacemaker. Zhen Dexiu of West Mountain said, "Anshi was in charge of the government for sixteen years. In the beginning he put a stop to the powerful ministers' schemes for usurpation; in the end he broke a powerful enemy's blades of annexation. His achievements were outstanding indeed! Even so, Anshi never planned for fame or gain; his lofty mentality and noble standards were akin to the likes of Kongming[56] and Zifang."[57]

Taoist Character

YANG XI

Yang Xi was styled Yihe. He was a man of Wu prefecture, but he moved his household to Jurong. He was born in 330. As a boy he was already in communication with the supernatural. He was handsome, good at conversation and humor, skilled at calligraphy and painting, as famous as Wang Xizhi. Xu Mai and Xu Mu, though much older, formed

53. Huan Wen (312–373) was an outstanding general of the Jin dynasty whose aspirations and ambitions brought him into conflict with the imperial court.
54. Fu Jian (338–385) was the third ruler (r. 357–385) of the Former Qin dynasty, founded by his grandfather in northern China in 351. Former Qin was one of the so-called Sixteen Kingdoms ruled by neighboring Asian peoples that established jurisdiction over parts of northern China in the fourth and fifth centuries C.E.
55. Wen Jiao served the Jin dynasty with distinction in both civil and military capacities. He was a leader in the suppression of two rebellions, including the revolt of Su Jun.
56. That is, Zhuge Liang, the great civil and military leader of the Three Kingdoms period.
57. That is, Zhang Liang, who helped to overthrow the Qin dynasty and establish the Han dynasty.

spiritual friendships with him early on. When Emperor Jianwen was king of Langye, he advanced to the position of counselor in chief. Through the recommendation of Xu Mu he became secretary of the royal office.

Then when Jianwen became emperor, Yang no longer sought promotion but took the high road, disregarding worldly success, meditating to elicit mystical experiences.

In 349 he received Zhonghuangzi's[58] method of controlling tigers and leopards. The next year the *Five Talismans* of the Spiritual Jewel teachings[59] was transmitted to him by Madame Wei's[60] eldest son Liu Pu. He was twenty-one years old at the time.

In the sixth month of the year 365, he moved the First Lady of the Purple Void, the Lady of the Lilac,[61] and Mistress An of Nine Flowers[62] to come down into his home, or sometimes to the mountain lodge of the administrator [Xu Mu]. That lodge was on Maoshan. He recorded scriptures and statements they transmitted and showed these to the masters Xu, father and son; so now he had become the administrator's scripture-transmitting teacher.

Mistress An of Nine Flowers took the opportunity to be his companion. She once told him, "Enlightened Master, you have pacified your disposition, empty and free; your secret house shines like jade, the fragrant pond flows high, your purity resounds in the Golden Palace. That is to say, you capably prize what is valuable and conceal

---

58. Zhonghuangzi was a legendary wizard who is supposed to have been consulted by the Yellow Emperor.

59. *The Spiritual Jewel* teachings means the Lingbao scriptures; the *Five Talismans* is one of the most important of the Lingbao scriptures.

60. Madame Wei was Wei Huacun, a famous female immortal. The First Lady of the Purple Void was an honorific bestowed on her by the emperor during the Tang dynasty. She had passed away decades before Yang Xi claimed to have contacted her. See *Lidai shenxian chuan* 8, and *Twilight Goddess* by Sartaz Aziz and Thomas Cleary (2000), p. 109 et passim.

61. The Lady of the Lilac is said to have been the twentieth daughter of the Matriarch of the West, a mythologized immortal associated with the Kunlun Mountains. The legends of the matriarch appear to have evolved out of contacts with central Asian shamanesses. Cf. *Lidai shenxian chuan* 8.

62. Mistress An is identified as the youngest daughter of a certain Mrs. Li, another immortalized woman. Cf. *Lidai shenxian chuan* 8. For Mrs. Li, see *Zhen Gao* in *Daozang jiyao*, vol. 18, p. 8033a. For accounts of these seminal séances, including a fuller list of visitants, cf. *Zhen Gao*, p. 7907 et passim.

the extraordinary; obscuring your reality, you shine within. You write out spiritual works, you harmonize with life according to natural processes, you purify your character in the garden of spirit, you make alchemical elixir and gold broth in the heaven of jade purity, you send up incense smoke that makes the sunlight disappear, in the darkness you drum a distant note. It is certain that you will work for great men thrice: you will attend the emperor in person, give eminent assistance to the imperial cabinet, and administer the system of a sage ruler. Regulating life and deciding death, rewarding and punishing ghosts and spirits, holding the fate of a thousand souls, sealing off mountains and summoning clouds, supervising the combined energies of yin and yang, you will be appointed the ruler of the ghosts and spirits of Wu and Yue. There's a constant refrain in the Three Offices, 'The great rulers Yang and An govern the realized and command the spirits.' This refers to us. You will mount a dragon and ride the clouds, ascending to heaven in broad daylight. If you cannot stand the smoke of wind-driven fire and wish to embrace your real form in hidden forests, then you should seek the path of sword release, to perform the art of apparent death. But if you faithfully dedicate yourself to the proper timing of engagement and silence, concealment and appearance, in appropriate places according to the time, there is a position of responsibility for an enlightened master."

Master Wang, president of the realized of West City, also taught him a method of taking in the light of the sun and moon.[63] Emperor Jianwen followed him as a teacher. He passed away in 386, at the age of fifty-seven.

In the Xuanhe era [1119–1125] of the Song dynasty an imperial rescript declared, "We are attentive to the celestial government and gaze on the views from the dragon terrace. Looking to the excellent spiritual homeland, we are anxious for mystic instruction in the nine flowers; admiring the precedents of successive immortals, we highlight the merits of their teaching. The realized man Yang, assistant director of destinies on East Flower Mountain, accumulated learning and clarified the subtle, polished his mind and merged with the infinite; he got the secret of Zhonghuang, received esoteric transmissions from realized ones of the South, governed the territories of Wu and

---

63. For methods of taking in the light of the sun and moon, see *Yunji qiqian* in *Daozang jiyao*, vol. 19, pp. 8606–7.

Yue, and managed the critical affairs of spirits and souls. Now he is famed on the Supreme Way and should be lauded with an exalted name, in hopes of reflection in the unbiased mirror and eternal abundance of gifts of many blessings. He is to be specially entitled the Realized Man of Clear Soul and Manifest Influence."

Xu Mu

Xu Mu was styled Sixuan. Another name of his was Mi. He was a man of Pingyu in Runan. His sixth-generation forefather Guang had moved his residence to Danyang.

He was born in 305. He graduated from the university with a doctorate and was assigned the post of magistrate of Yuyao, then summoned by imperial command to be a secretarial court gentleman, then transferred to prefecture personnel manager, administrator of the Central Defense Force, and senior recorder of the Imperial Secretariat.

While outwardly involved in worldly work, he inwardly cultivated the study of reality. He used to look up to the lofty example of his elder brother Yuanyou, so when Emperor Jianwen died, he concentrated on quietude in a mountain cottage.

He had a deep spiritual association with Master Yang, and when a group of the realized descended upon Yang, all of their scriptures and statements were transmitted to Xu Mu. He was liberated and sublimated in 376, at the age of seventy-one. His sons and nephews ceremoniously entombed an empty casket in a large grave west of the suburbs.

Declarations of the Realized says, "His mastery was based on an outstanding destiny; his heritage was already ancient, namely, a younger brother of the Duke of Xue in the time of King Wu of Zhou, plus the merit bequeathed by the founding of the state of Xu,[64] which also shed corresponding blessings on descendants; so he was born to fortune and attained the Way based on his natural disposition. Granted a jade certificate, he became a realized human of higher purity. His ranks reached those of marquis and earl, while his offices included

---

64. According to traditional genealogy, the surname Xu was taken from the state of Xu, where the ancestor of the clan was enfeoffed by King Wu of the Zhou dynasty. The pedigree of the Xus was thus intimately connected with the foundation of the Zhou, which was the model dynasty for Confucian political and moral philosophy.

minister and director. Regulating immortals, he governed with care; assisting sages, he shepherded the people."

An imperial proclamation of the Xuanhe era [1119–1125] says, "We have caused the jade mirror of the president of the realized ones to descend and have ascended the dragon terrace of shining light. Here we impart order to the retinue of mystics so as to bring relief to people on earth below. Whoever shows merit of a Taoist type is promoted to office in the clan of immortals. Administrator Xu, Real Human of Higher Purity, was pure and simple, outwardly harmonious, having inwardly attained spiritual enlightenment. The voice of his soul was beautifully expressed. Personally participating in the parties of sages, floating up and roaming transcendent, he assisted the order of higher purity above. Now that he has gone to heaven, he should be honored with a virtuous name, in hopes he may manifest assistance to increase the spread of effortless government. He is to be specially entitled Real Human of Great Nothingness Spreading Virtue."

Xu Hui

Xu Hui was styled Daoxiang. When he was young he was nicknamed Jade Axe. He was the third son of the administrator [Xu Mu]. His purity was exceptional, clear and unblemished, quite beyond the standards of the world. He was born in 341.

The prefecture recommended him for accounts assistant, recorder, exemplary minister of education, and senior archive clerk, but he did not take up any of these offices. He built a house in front of Mount Leiping, an extension of Juqu [Maoshan], and privately practiced the higher path. In 365 the Lady of the Lilac came down to teach; thenceforth he exchanged letters with a number of realized people and thoroughly practiced the methods of returning to the source,[65] flying walking,[66] and the two lights of the sun and moon.[67] He used to wish

65. See *Shangqing Taishang huiyuan yindao chuzui jijing* and *Shangqing Taishang huiyuan jiudao feixing yujing*.

66. See *Taishang feibu wuxing jing*. See also *Taishan kongchang feibu lu*, in *Daozang jiyao*, vol. 19, p. 8613a.

67. *Yilin* is a contraction of *yuyi jielin; yuyi* means "sunlight," *jielin* refers to the moon. Cf. *Zhen Gao*, in *Daozang jiyao*, vol. 18, pp. 7934b and 8030a; also *Yunji qiqian*, in *Daozang jiyao*, vol. 19, pp. 8603–4.

he could roam the caves as soon as possible; he didn't want to stay in the human world for long. In 370 he went to the north cave and ostensibly died; he was thirty years old at the time.

The story told by old-timers says, "The clerk lit incense and prostrated himself at the stone altar in the north cave. He remained prostrate and did not rise. The next morning, when they looked at his body, it was like he was alive." The younger master Mao gave out a statement that Mr. Xu had left his body and mystically sublimated, following the nocturnal liberation of Zhang Zhennan. Zhennan was the third-generation Celestial Teacher Zhang Lu.[68]

After this, Xu lived in a marginal cave dwelling and used to come to the square terrace. *Declarations of the Realized* says he would pass through Donghua[69] and become an immortal of noble higher purity. This is the one whom the Recluse [Tao Hongjing] calls the Teacher of Reality with the Mystery.

In the Xuanhe era [1119–1125] he was entitled the Real Human Merged into Elemental Unity. The pronouncement said, "The purple absolute permeates the elemental; though undifferentiated in one energy, the register of ranking in the alchemical state actually organizes the status of myriad realized ones. Anyone elevated to rank in the religion of immortals has done great service at the outset of the path. The realized human Xu of Donghua, Immortal Noble of Higher Purity, Attendant to the Divine, refined the three spirits[70] to gaze into the subtle, stabilized the nine latitudes to excel.[71] He ostensibly died in the north cave, betaking himself to the abode of hidden people; treading the scenery of Donghua, he crossed over alone on the highest form of journey. Even though he loftily refused worldly fame, his will was set on benevolent protection. We still hope he sends down assistance, to expand the great network."

---

68. Zhang Lu was a grandson of the first Celestial Teacher, Zhang Ling (Zhang Daoling). See *Sanguozhi, Weishu* 8.

69. A center of esoteric Taoist government.

70. According to the teaching of the *Huangdingjing*, the three spirits are the elemental spirit, the conscious spirit, and the real spirit.

71. Here the *nine latitudes* refers to the system of passes or openings used in Taoist yoga, with three parallel sets of three points along energy channels up the spine, the center of the torso, and the front of the torso.

A Taoist Recluse

Liu Linzhi

Liu Linzhi was styled Ziqi, and also Yiming. He was a man of Nanyang.[72] In youth he valued simplicity; he was retiring and had few desires. He didn't practice formal disciplines, and nobody knew him. He liked to wander in the mountains and wilds; his aspiration was to be free.

Once when he was gathering herbs on Mount Heng, he went so far in that he forgot how to get back. He came upon a valley stream. On the south side of the stream there were two big mushrooms; one mushroom was closed, the other was open. The stream was too deep and wide to cross.

Someone told him there are all sorts of substances in mushrooms used in prescriptions for immortality and wonder drugs, and Linzhi wanted to look for them again, but he could never find where they were anymore.

Whenever people gave him gifts, he would never accept anything.

More than a hundred *li* from Linzhi's house was an old widow who was sick and about to die. She lamented to people, "Who's going to bury me? There's only Administrator Liu. How will I let him know?" Linzhi had previously heard of her affliction, so he went to look in on her. Finding her life over, he personally provided a casket and funeral for her. That's how humane, caring, and sympathetic he was.

One day he heard that a fisherman of Wuling Valley had found his way into Peach Blossom Spring.[73] Delighted, he wanted to go but died before he fulfilled the quest.

The record in *Tao the Sought-After Scholar*[74] praises him as an eminent gentleman; surely we can imagine his personality.

---

72. In Henan.
73. A sort of Shangri-la of Chinese literature, to which people are said to have fled from the rigors of the regime of the First Emperor of China. The native inhabitants were said to dress like "foreigners" and to have blond hair. Chinese literary sources place it in Hunan, while blond hair suggests people of central Asian origin. See *The Mummies of Urumchi* by Elizabeth Wayland Barber (1999).
74. This is an abbreviated title of a composition about Tao Qian (Tao Yuanming, 365–427), considered one of the greatest poets in Chinese history, written by his friend Yan Yanzhi.

Taoist Arts

SU XI

Su Xi was a man of Dunhuang.[75] Empty and serene, he was fond of study and did not accept appointments from the province and prefecture. He was recommended in the categories of *filial and honest* and *chief of the wise and good*, but he refused both on the pretext of illness. He thought freely about the arts of yin and yang and wrote more than ten works on astronomy and topography, which were very instructive.

Zhang Moushi and Yin Dan, governor of Dunhuang, considered him extraordinary and went to visit him, neglecting to return for days on end. When he died of illness at the age of seventy-nine, Dan went to his funeral in white silk mourning clothes and donated twenty thousand in cash. Dan said, "What worldly people have in excess is wealth and status; what the eyes like is color, what the ears like is music. But the maestro discarded what most people keep and kept what most people discard. He savored the flavorless in a state of ecstasy, included multiple layers of mystery with myriad marvels. His residence didn't cover a single *mou*, but his will made little of the nine provinces. His body resided in the realm of worldly convention, but he rested his mind beyond the heavens. Even the lofty remoteness of Qian Lou,[76] or the indifference of Chuang-tzu, did not surpass him."

He was given the posthumous name Maestro of the Mysterious Abode.

A Taoist Recluse

ZHANG ZHONG

Zhang Zhong was styled Chenhe. He was a man of Zhongshan.[77] With the disturbance of the Yonghe era [307–313] he went into seclu-

---

75. In Gansu, an important center of contact between China and central Asia since the Han dynasty.

76. Qian Lou was a high-minded gentleman pauper of the Spring and Autumn era, noted for rejecting appointments to high office in two feudal states.

77. Zhongshan is a place name in Hebei, but it is also the name of a number of mountains. The closest of these latter to Mount Tai, the sacred mountain in Shandong where Zhang went into seclusion, containing the second of thirty-six minor grotto heavens of Taoist topography, would be Zhongshan in Jiangsu.

sion on Mount Tai. He was taciturn and had few desires. Clear and empty, he did breathing exercises, ate pine nuts, and ingested atracty- lodes and practiced energy-induction exercises. He didn't study the classics; the doctrine he promoted was based solely on the empty nothingness of the Supreme Way.

Living in clustered crags and deep valleys, he'd dig a hole in the ground to make a burrow. His disciples also lived in burrows, at least sixty paces from his, visiting him once every five days. He taught physically, not verbally; his disciples learning practices would ob- serve him and withdraw.

He set up a Taoist altar over his burrow and bowed at it every morning. He used an earthen vessel for meals and hollowed out a stone for a pot. When people living in the vicinity would give him clothes and food, he'd never accept anything. When the curious would ask him about omens of water and fire, Zhong would say, "The sky does not speak, yet the four seasons go on therein, and myriad be- ings are born therein. Matters of yin and yang are not within the knowledge of this poor old rustic." This is how he would dismiss ex- ternal things.

At the age of one hundred, his seeing and hearing were still accu- rate. Fu Jian[78] sent an envoy to invite him, presenting him with a robe and hat. He declined, saying, "I'm decrepit and balding; I can't wear a robe and hat. Let me meet in my country clothes."

Jian said to him, "Maestro, you stay in mountain forests research- ing and refining the elements of the Way; your individual goodness is more than enough but not your assistance to society. That is why I've importuned you from afar; I will appoint you father figure of Qi."

Zhong said, "A long time ago I fled the land to Mount Tai on account of destructive disorder, making birds and beasts my companions, to live out my evanescent life. Even if it were an era of a sage leader like Yao or Shun, I've deteriorated with age and my will is gone—I cannot be effective in the role of father figure. It's not that I dare to affect the nature of a mountain dweller, but my feelings remain in the crags, so I beg to return for my remaining years, going back to die on Mount Tai."

Jian sent him off in a comfortable carriage. When the entourage reached Mount Hua, he lamented, "I am a Taoist of the East Mountain

---

78. Fu Jian was then ruler of the Former Qin dynasty.

[Mount Tai] dying on the West Mountain [Mount Hua]. It's fate—what can one do?" They traveled fifty *li*, then when they reached the pass he died.

The envoy raced back to report this. Jian sent the palace gentleman Wei Hua with a document of recognition, funereal offerings, and ceremonial clothing. Jian gave Zhang Zhong the posthumous title Maestro at Peace on the Way.

A Taoist Scholar

SONG XIAN

Song Xian was styled Lingwen. He was a man of Xiaogu in Dunhuang. When he was young he had far-reaching discipline; steeped in serenity, he didn't mingle with society. He lived in seclusion in the mountains south of Wine Springs, studying the classics and the parallels. More than three thousand students took lessons from him.

The governor of Wine Springs, Ma Ji, was a high-minded gentleman; he paid a visit in full ceremony, sounding bells and drums, but Xian stayed inside, refusing to see him. Ji lamented, "The maestro's name is to be heard, but his person is not to be seen; his virtue is to be admired, but his appearance cannot be ascertained. I know the maestro is a dragon among men." He inscribed a poem on a stone wall saying:

> Cinnabar cliffs a hundred feet high,
> Azure walls ten thousand fathoms;
> Outstanding trees flourish,
> Luxurious as the forest of Deng.[79]
> The man is like jade,
> A treasure of the nation.
> The house is near but the man is far;
> I've really worn out my heart.

79. A mythical forest. The book of *Lieh-tzu* says, "Father Kua, not assessing his own strength, wanted to chase the sunlight and pursued it to the horizon. He got so thirsty he drank up the Yellow River and the Wei River. The Yellow River and the Wei River weren't sufficient, so he headed north to drink the great lake. Before he arrived, however, he died of thirst on the way. The staff he left behind, infused with the fat and flesh of his body, sprouted the Deng Forest. The Deng Forest is thousands of miles in size."

When Song Xian died he was eighty-three. He was posthumously entitled Maestro of Mystic Emptiness.

Taoist Silence

TAO TAN

Tao Tan was styled Chujing. He was a grandson of Chief Defender Kan.[80] Orphaned when young, he liked the arts of energy induction and cultivation and considered the path of immortality within reach. When he was fifteen or sixteen years old he was already taking elixirs and abstaining from grain. He never married.

His family was rich, with hundreds of servants and dependents, but Tan did nothing all day long, never getting involved in management. He was quite fond of reading the *I Ching* and good at divination. He built a hermitage on Mount Linxiang in Changsha[81] and lived there; he raised a white deer as a companion to keep him company. If relatives or old acquaintances tried to look in on him, he'd move to the other side of a valley stream so no one could get near him.

When the province recommended him for examination in the category of *outstanding ability*, Tan then moved away to the hills of Luoxian,[82] never to return. No one knows where he ended up.

A Taoist Recluse

TAO QIAN

Tao Qian was styled Yuanming. He was a great-grandson of Tao Kan. He was high-minded from youth; he studied widely and was a good writer. He was extraordinary and unbridled, natural and self-possessed.

He once wrote "The Story of Mr. Five Willows" describing himself: "I don't know where he's from, and I'm not sure what his name is. There are five willow trees around his house, so I call him Mr. Five Willows. He's calm and taciturn, with no ambition for glory or gain. He

---

80. Tao Kan (259–334), a distinguished governor and military commander in the service of the Jin dynasty.
81. In Hunan.
82. In Hunan.

likes reading books but doesn't seek too much interpretation; whenever he gets a hint, he's so elated he forgets to eat. He's fond of wine by nature, but he's poor and cannot always obtain it. His relatives and friends know this, so they sometimes set out wine and invite him; he goes and drinks it up at once, staying long enough to get drunk and then, once drunk, retiring, never caring about leaving or staying. His cottage is quiet but doesn't keep out wind and sun. His short woolens are worn through and stitched, he repeatedly runs out of food and drink, and yet he is at peace. He is always writing for his own pleasure, showing something of his individual will. Forgetting thoughts of gain and loss, he'll end on his own this way.

"Qian Lou had a saying:

" 'Not disturbed by poverty or lowliness,
Not hurried by wealth and status.'
The epitome of that saying is here,
In the likes of this man!
He entertains his mind
With intoxication and poetry;
Is he of the clan of Mr. Mindless?
Is he of the people of Getian?" [83]

His own preface was like this; people of the time thought it was a true account.

Because his great-grandfather had been a minister of the Jin dynasty, Tao Qian considered it a disgrace to subordinate himself to a subsequent dynasty, so he never served in government again after the founder of the Song dynasty rose to royalty [420–423]. His writings are all dated: before the Yixi era of Jin [405–419], the year era of the Jin dynasty is clearly written; after the Yongchu era of Song [420–423] only the cyclic notation of years is recorded.

He once said he was lying under a north-facing window in the fifth or sixth month when a cool breeze gradually came up and he thought he was the august ruler Fuxi.[84]

83. An idealized prehistoric leader said to have been trusted implicitly and followed without persuasion.
84. An idealized leader and culture hero of high antiquity, associated with the origin of the I Ching.

He died in 427 at the age of sixty-three. Yan Yannian composed his eulogy. He was posthumously entitled Sought-After Scholar of Calm Conduct.

Taoist Character

LU XIUJING

Lu Xiujing was styled Yuanji. He was a man of Dongqian in Wuxing.[85] His father Lin was recruited nine times by the government but never rose to the summons; he was given the posthumous name Purist of the High Road. The maestro Xiujing had double circles on the soles of his feet, double ankle bones on his legs, the character *great* on his palms, and star patterns on his back. He was devoted to literature and also studied symbols and parallels. When he grew up, he was fond of unconventional journeys. He went south to Mount Heng, the Xiang River, and Mount Jiuyi[86] visiting the relics of the realized ones of the South; he went west to Emei[87] and West City,[88] following the lofty trail of purity and emptiness.

Later in the Yuanhe era [424–454] of Song, he was selling herbs in the capital. Emperor Wen summoned him, but he didn't go, instead returning to Mount Lu[89] on this account. In 467 Emperor Ming commissioned Wang Jingzong, inspector of Jiangzhou, to formally invite him to come to court. He was lodged in the posterior palace by imperial command.

The emperor also ordered a gathering at the Lodge for Savants in Flowering Forest Park. When the royalty and nobility had assembled, the maestro came up and greeted the emperor in deerskin. The emperor silently increased his respect. Subsequently, Shu Jizhen having obtained the doctrines of the scriptures of Higher Purity of the realized ones Yang and Xu, the emperor ordered that they be entrusted to the maestro, as religious leader of the age, to compile a tripartite canon.

85. In Zhejiang.
86. Mount Heng, the Xiang River, and Mount Jiuyi are all in Hunan, which means "south of the lake."
87. Emei, in Sichuan, is the westernmost of the five sacred mountains, containing the seventh of the thirty-six minor grotto heavens of Taoism.
88. Third of the Ten Great Grotto Heavens, or major cave centers, of Taoism.
89. Mount Lu in Jiangxi contains the eighth of the thirty-six minor grotto heavens.

The emperor also ordered that the Lodge for Honoring Emptiness be built on Mount Tianyin north of the capital, to be a religious center for transmission of the scriptures.

The next year the emperor fell ill and went to this lodge to perform a divinely ordained purification rite. One evening a yellow vapor shaped like a precious parasol covered the sanctuary, and the emperor had a strange dream; then he began to recover from his illness.

In 477, suddenly the maestro started preparing to go back to the mountains as before; his disciples all wondered about this. Then on the second day of the third month he unexpectedly passed away. The emperor ordained that his hat and shoes be sent to be kept in the Taoist monastery of Simplicity and Silence, and he was posthumously named Maestro of Simplicity and Silence.

In the Xuanhe era [1119–1125] he was given the title Realized Man of the Cinnabar Base.

Taoist Sayings

DONG JING

Dong Jing was styled Weinian. It is not known what province he was from. He first showed up on Luoyang with the accounts officer of Longxi. He went about with his hair unkempt, singing as he meandered, always lodging in Baishe [outside Luoyang]. Sun Chu[90] was writing in those days and went to Baishe a number of times to talk to him. Several years later he disappeared, and no one knew where he'd gone. Where he used to sleep there was nothing but a wild pink and two poems.

One poem said:

> The Way of the Creative is firm and simple,
> The body of the Receptive is warm and intimate.[91]
> Though indistinct, the cosmic elemental
> Is a model to be followed.
> Latter-day society, rushing with the current,
> Replaces substance with embellishment;
> Worldly affairs that go on and on—

90. Sun Chu (d. 293) was a noted poet.
91. *The Creative* and *the Receptive* refer to the first two symbols of the *I Ching*.

Who knows their reality?
Fleeing, I'm going home from here to emptiness,
Returning to my natural abode.

The other poem said:

Confucius never had his day,
But he attracted a unicorn;
Why didn't he escape society
To preserve reality?

Taoist Influence

DAN DAOKAI

Dan Daokai was a man of Dunhuang. He always wore coarse wool, and whenever he was given gifts of silk clothing he'd never wear it. He didn't fear cold or heat and didn't lie down day or night.

He used to ingest tiny pebbles, swallowing several at once, once a day, sometimes more and sometimes less.[92] He liked living in the mountains; the spirits of the mountain forests appeared in strange forms to test him, but he never showed any sign of fear.

In the time of Shi Jilong,[93] Dan came from Xiping, traveling hundreds of miles in a day. When he got to Qin province he reported his arrival in Ye;[94] Jilong had Fotuteng[95] talk with him, and he couldn't

---

92. The account of Dan's diet is more detailed in the Buddhist collection *Stories of Eminent Monks*, where it is noted that he gave up grain and ate cedar nuts. When cedar nuts could not be obtained, the story continues, he would ingest pine sap. It was after this that he took to swallowing pebbles, but even then the Buddhist account says he would sometimes chew some ginger or prickly ash peppers. His immunity to cold and heat were acquired after seven years of this regime. After ten years, Dan was the only one of ten fellow practitioners who had not died or given up the discipline. *Gaosengchuan chuji* 10.

93. Shi Jilong proclaimed himself emperor of the Later Zhao dynasty in 349.

94. The capital of Later Zhao.

95. Fotuteng was a Buddhist monk from central Asia, particularly famous for supernatural powers. Dan Daokai is also listed as a Buddhist in *Stories of Eminent Monks*, and this name is Buddhist in form. His lay surname was Meng, the same as the famous philosopher Mencius. His native Dunhuang was an important Buddhist center; construction on Buddhist cave shrines there began in 366.

stump him. Fotuteng said, "This Taoist observes the rise and fall of the state—if he leaves, there will be chaos." When Jilong was in decline, Daokai crossed south into Xucheng, and chaos erupted in Ye.

In 359 he went to the capital city [of the Eastern Jin dynasty]; later he went to Nanhai and went into Mount Luofu, where he lived alone in a thatch hut tranquilly, beyond things. He was more than one hundred years old when he passed away in his mountain dwelling.

He instructed his disciples to place his corpse in a stone cavern, so they moved him into a cave. When Ai Hong of Chen prefecture became governor of Nanhai, he climbed Mount Luofu and got to the mouth of that cave. He saw Daokai's remains; he looked like he was still alive. His incense burner and earthen vessel were still there. The governor sighed, "The master's practice was exceptional; it's just as if he simply molted." So then he composed a eulogy for him.

[7]

SOUTHERN DYNASTIES
(420–588)

A Taoist Recluse

ZONG PING

Zong Ping was styled Shaowen. He was a man of Nanyang.

When the future Emperor Wu of Song [r. 420–422] had executed Liu
Yi[1] and taken over Xing province, he asked Yi's consultant Shen Yong,
"What measures are appropriate for the present day?"

Yong said, "Eliminate longstanding antagonisms, increase charity
and welfare, organize clan ranks, and distinguish and select the talented and able. That's all."

Emperor Wu took this advice and appointed Ping to the office of
recorder, but he wouldn't take the job. When the emperor asked him
why, he replied, "After living in the hills and drinking from valley
streams for more than thirty years, how can I stoop to being a flunky?"
The emperor thought that was a good reply and dropped the matter.

Ping was superb at the lute, drew diagrams and painted, and was an
expert linguist. Whenever he went roaming the mountains and rivers,
as soon as he'd go he'd forget to come back.

When Ping's older brother Cang became governor of Nanping, he
pressured Ping to come back with him. So he built a house by the three
lakes of Jiangling and lived there at ease, without concerns. Emperor
Wu tried to recruit him to become general adviser to the infantry of
the chief defender, and Empress Yu appointed him to be a secretary,

---

1. Liu Yi (d. 412) joined with Liu Yu (363–422) against the warlord Huan Xuan
(369–404), who usurped the throne of Jin and set up the Chu dynasty. Liu Yu, who
was to become Emperor Wu of Song, subsequently turned on Liu Yi and forced him to
commit suicide.

but he didn't take either office. When the king of Hengyang, Yi Ji, went to Xing province, he personally went to Ping's house and drank with him. He appointed him consultant, but after all he didn't take the job.

He was fond of mountains and waters and liked to go on distant journeys. To the west he climbed Xing[2] and Wu[3] mountains; in the south he scaled Mount Heng. He returned to Jiangling on account of illness. He lamented, "Old age and sickness have arrived together; I'm afraid I won't be able to tour all the famous mountains. I'll just clarify my heart and visualize the way, traveling there lying down." He drew pictures of all the places he'd traveled on the walls.

He used to tell people, "I'm inclined to play drum and lute, to make the mountains echo." In the past there was percussion music favored by the Huans; when the Huan clan perished, that music died out, transmitted only by Ping. Emperor Wen sent his music master Yang Huan to learn it from him.

Taoist Scholarship

SHEN DAOJIAN

Shen Daojian was a man of Wukang in Wuxing. As a youth he was kind and loving and fond of the *Lao-tzu* and the *I Ching.* He lived in a cloister below rocky mountains in the north of the prefecture, sharing his livelihood with orphaned nephews, never changing his discipline on account of hardship.

He learned the lute from Dai Kui and Wang Jinglong, who deeply respected him. He was offered official appointments by the province twelve times, but he declined them all.

Once when someone was stealing from his garden, he returned from outside and saw him. He immediately concealed himself, waiting for the thief to leave before coming out. Another time someone was digging up the big bamboo shoots from behind his house. He had someone put a stop to this, saying, "Let's spare these shoots so they can become a forest; there'll be even better ones to give you." Then he sent him to buy big shoots to give the man, but the thief was too em-

2. In Shaanxi.
3. In Sichuan.

barrassed to take them. So Daojian had him leave them in his yard and go home.

Village youths used to come to take lessons from him, but Daojian never had any food to support disciples, so Kong Jinzhi, the prefect of Wukang, provided ample support, enabling all the students to achieve some success. Emperor Wen [r. 424–453] heard of this and sent an envoy to pay a courtesy call.

Daojian was still living on coarse fare even in his old age, never having enough to get by on, but he enjoyed music and calligraphy and continued to practice them diligently. After he died his son Huifeng practiced those arts, never accepting official appointments.

Taoist Recluses

LIU NINGZHI

Liu Ningzhi was styled Yin-an [or Zhi-an]. He was a man of Jijiang in Nanjun.[4] Aspiring to be a person like Lao Lai[5] and Yan Ziling, he gave his family fortune to his younger brother and nephew, built a cottage in the wilds, and refused to eat anything he had not worked for.

Provincial and local authorities respected his virtuous conduct, and they tried to recruit him, but he never accepted office. The king of Linguan, Wang Yi, and the king of Hengyang, Yi Ji, both sent envoys to ask after him. In Ningzhi's letters of reply he referred to himself humbly but without practicing the custom of commoners, so some people criticized him about this. Ningzhi said, "In ancient times Lao Lai addressed himself to the king of Chu this way, and Yan Ling also refused courtesies to Emperor Guangwu; I've never heard of Chao Fu or Xu You calling themselves 'subjects' to Yao or Shun."

That year there were food shortages in Jingzhou, and Yi Ji was worried that Ningzhi might starve to death, so he presented him with a hundred thousand cash. Delighted, Ningzhi took the cash to the market gate and gave some to anyone he saw looking hungry; within a very short time he had given it all away.

He had a natural fondness for mountains and waters. One day he took his wife and children and went off sailing on the rivers and lakes,

---

4. In Hubei.
5. Lao Lai is sometimes identified with Laozi.

living thereafter in seclusion on the south side of Mount Heng. Climbing up to a high ridge, beyond human tracks, he made a small cottage and lived there, spending the rest of his life gathering herbs and consuming them.

CHU BOYU

Chu Boyu was styled Yuanqu. He was a man of Qiantang in Wujun. He had the discipline of a recluse in youth, with few habitual desires. When he was eighteen years old his parents arranged a marriage for him, but when his wife came in the front door, Boyu went out the back door. Subsequently he went into Shan[6] and lived on Waterfall Mountain.

He was naturally able to withstand cold and heat; people of the time compared him to Wang Zhongdou.[7] He stayed in the mountains for more than thirty years, utterly secluded from human beings.

When Wang Sengjian worked for Wujun county, he invited Boyu with excruciating courtesy, until he couldn't refuse. He stayed over at the county seat for two nights, exchanged a few words, and then left. When Emperor Gao assumed the throne [in 479], he personally commanded the counties of Wu and Hui to invite him formally, but he refused this too, claiming illness.

The emperor didn't want to importune him anymore, so he ordered the construction of the Lodge of Great Peace on White Stone Mountain in Shan prefecture to house him. He died when he was eighty-six years old. Boyu always lived upstairs, so he was buried on the building grounds. Kong Gui,[8] who had received Taoist teachings from him, set up a memorial tablet for him by the side of the lodge.

Taoist Scholarship

GU HUAN

Gu Huan was styled Jingyi. Another style of his was Xuannian. He was a man of Yanguan in Wujun.

---

6. In Zhejiang.
7. A Taoist of the first century B.C.E., said to have lived more than two hundred years.
8. A scholar, writer, and government official.

He already knew how to figure an astrological system when he was only six or seven years old.

His family was poor. His father sent him to the fields to chase birds; he composed an elegy on orioles and came back home. The birds had eaten half the grain, and his father was so angry he was going to beat him but stopped when he read the elegy.

There was a school in his district, but Huan was too poor to afford lessons, so he'd listen in from behind the school building, never forgetting anything. At night he'd burn pine knots to read, or else he'd burn bran for his light.

When he grew up, his devotion never slackened. He heard that Shao Xuanzhi of Dongxian in Wuxing was able to transmit the readings of the Five Classics, so he temporarily made him his literature teacher and took lessons from him. When he was twenty-something years old, he also inquired into the doctrines of mysticism and scholarship[9] from Lei Cizong[10] of Yuzhang.

When his mother died, he didn't even drink water for six or seven days, camping by the grave. Subsequently he lived in seclusion and didn't serve in government. He opened a school on Mount Tiantai in Shan prefecture and gathered students; there were always nearly a hundred taking lessons.

He was naturally fond of Huang-Lao and took dietary supplements, but he never told anyone about it. Every morning he'd go outdoors, and the mountain birds would gather and take food from his palm.

He also understood the books on yin and yang, and his calculations often proved accurate.

There was a strange illness recurrent in Whitestone Village in Shangyin. Villagers told Huan about it, seeking his sympathy. Huan then went to the village and lectured on Lao-tzu, and the afflicted all got well.

Another time when someone was troubled by an aberration, Huan was asked about it. Huan said, "What books are there in the house?" He answered, "Only the *Classic of Filial Piety*." Huan said, "Put Confucius beside the patient's pillow; if he respects it, he'll get well." The patient actually did get well. People asked how it was so. Huan replied,

9. That is, Taoism and Confucianism.
10. Lei Cizong (386–448) was a hermit recruited to teach Confucianism at the university established in 438 by Emperor Wen of the (Liu) Song dynasty (r. 424–454).

"Good chases out evil, rectitude triumphs over aberration. That is why the sickness abated."

Kong Gui once climbed up the mountain to call on Huan, and they discussed the Four Bases.[11] Huan said, "The principle of the center is but one—how could there be two? None of the four bases is correct, because they are missing the center." Then he wrote *Treatise on Three Terms* to correct this.

Huan was not an eloquent speaker, but he excelled in expository writing. He wrote notes on Wang Bi's two appendixes to the *I Ching;* students passed these on. He became recorder of Yangzhou after [future] emperor Gao of the Qi dynasty [r. 479–483] was assisting government; then when Emperor Gao assumed the throne, Huan came, calling himself a subject from the mountain valleys, and presented a book, *Outline of Government*. The emperor issued a commendation praising its excellence. When Huan returned east, he was presented with a simple lute strung with elk tail hairs.

When he knew he was dying, he composed a poem to express his will:

> There is no permanent home on the Five Roads;[12]
> There is a permanent abode in the Three Purities.[13]
> Vitality and energy operate by nature,
> The wandering soul evolves along with beings.
> Giant fish and giant birds go to the oceans,
> Cicadas and pigeons take to mulberry trees.
> When you master life, you may go or stay;
> When you're expert at death, you equalize day and night.
> Leaving it to destiny, you're secure in what you ride;
> Where can you not travel?
> Elevate your mind to aim for foreknowledge;
> Melt away from here.

He decided the day of his own death and chose the time of his own funeral. He died on Mount Shan at the age of sixty-four. His body was

---

11. Proposing that ability and nature are the same, or different, or conjoined, or separate.

12. A Buddhist term referring to the various states of being in the mundane world.

13. Three Taoist heavens, called jadelike purity, higher purity, and great purity.

fragrant and warm, so he must have been liberated from the corpse and become immortal.

He was sent back to be entombed in his ancestral grave. Two trees grew intertwined beside the tomb; the prefect Jian Shantu reported a description.

A Taoist Scholar

Du Jingchan

Du Jingchan was styled Jingqi. He was a man of Qiantang in Wujun. He was calm and quiet in youth and closed his mind to success and government service. He was widely read, but he concentrated on practicing Huang-Lao. He was good friends with Gu Huan[14] of the same prefecture and opened a school on East Mountain in Shining.[15]

In the beginning of the Jianwu era [494–498], he was recruited for the post of supernumerary gentleman cavalier attendant. Jingchan said, "When Chuang-tzu went fishing, would a white jade disk[16] have brought him back?" After all, he refused, giving illness as an excuse, and died without taking the position.

Taoist Character

Zong Ce

Zong Ce was styled Jing Wei. He was a grandson of Zong Ping, a distinguished gentleman whose services were sought by the Song dynasty. Ce was quiet and retiring in youth and did not enjoy human society. He used to lament, "When one's family is poor and one's parents are old, to serve in government, whatever the office, has been approved by philosophers of the past, but I have my doubts. If one really cannot affect the gold in the ground by occult means or mystically bring the carp in the rivers, one must only apply the guidance of nature and distribute

14. Gu Huan (420–483) was the author of *Yixialun,* an anti-Buddhist work whose title may be paraphrased as *Treatise on Foreigners and Chinese.* There are several critiques of this work in the Buddhist compendium *Hongmingji.*
15. In Zhejiang.
16. An emblematic accessory of a court official.

the yield of the earth. Who can consume an enormous salary from others and worry about the enormous problems of others?"

When the cavalry commander Yi, king of Yuzhang, tried to recruit him to be a consultant, Ce replied to the official summons, "Why mistakenly injure seabirds and wrongly topple mountain trees?"

The king of Yuzhang again sent a letter inviting him. Ce replied, "My nature is the same as the fish and birds'; I like to stay in mountains and valleys, enamored of the pines and clouds, and easily get lost on human roads. Free among the crags and streams, there is someone who seems insane; suddenly, unawares, old age has arrived, and now my hair is already white. How could I judge the have-nots and charge the haves, resent the fish and admire the birds?"

Wishing to travel to the famous mountains, he copied on the wall Shang Ziping's[17] map made by his grandfather Ping. Ce's eldest son Pin's official post was in the capital city; when he learned of his father's intentions, he asked for a stipend to go back to be chief of Nanjun; subsequently his father handed on the affairs of the family to him. Everyone from Inspector Wang Zidun of Anlu and Administrator Lin Yan on down sent him parting gifts, but Ce didn't accept anything. All he took with him were two books, *Lao-tzu* and *Chuang-tzu*. His children and grandchildren bowed farewell, weeping sadly, but Ce whistled all the while and didn't look at them.

Now he went to Mount Lu, where he stopped at his grandfather Ping's old house. The Marquis of Yufu, Zixiang, then governing Jiang province, sent him a generous gift. Ce said, "I've been afflicted by madness since youth, visiting mountains and gathering herbs, and have come a long way to get here. I eat pine nuts and atractylodes according to the size of my stomach and wear leaves according to the size of my body. However simple, this is already enough; how could I merit this extravagant expenditure?"

Zixiang commandeered a carriage to go to him, but Ce avoided him and would not meet him. He would only visit and converse with like-minded friends Yu Yi and Liu Jiu and his clansman Shangzhi. In 495 he was summoned by the emperor to be recorder for the Ministry of Education, but he didn't accept the post. Then he died.

Ce was good at painting. He personally made a picture on a screen

17. Shang Chang, a recluse who refused government service. A notice of him is found in the *Book of the Latter Han*.

of Ruan Ji meeting Sun Deng, and sat and reclined facing it. He was also good at music and versed in the *I Ching* and *Lao-tzu*. He wrote a three-volume continuation of Huangfu Mi's *Stories of Eminent Men*. He also wrote accounts of Mount Heng and Mount Lu.

A Taoist Scholar

SHEN LINSHI

Shen Linshi was styled Yunzhen. He was a man of Wukang in Wuxing. He was exceptionally quick as a boy. Hearing his uncle Yue quoting assorted sayings of mystics, he remembered them all perfectly. Yue patted him on the shoulder and said, "If this culture is not to die out, it will reside in you, it seems!"

By the time he grew up, he had become broadly conversant with the classics and histories, but he was high-minded and lived unknown in a local valley. His family was poor, and he made a living by weaving blinds while ceaselessly reciting books. Local people called him Professor Blind-Weaver.

He was well versed in the traditions on manners and personally instructed the locals in vernacular. When he was urged to go into government service, he replied, "Fish are hooked, animals are penned. When the world is one in agreement, sages mystically sense it; that is why they always act with felicitous prospects. I really am as yet unable to effectively practice sitting forgetting; why don't I aim for daily reduction?"[18] Then he composed "Elegy on Mystic Freedom" to refuse the suggestion.

He lectured on classics and gave instruction. Several dozen to a hundred took lessons from him, each building a house to reside by him. People of the time said of this, "There is a savant in the Wuqiang Mountains who has opened a school and teaches, the residents a veritable city."

Some of his clansmen, such as Yuan, director of the Ministry of Personnel, and Yue, gentleman of the Imperial Secretariat, submitted a statement of recommendation of Linshi's righteous conduct, and he

18. The expression *daily reduction* comes from the *Tao Te Ching:* "For learning, you increase daily; for the Way you reduce daily. Reducing and reducing, you thereby reach nonstriving. Though there is no striving, nothing is undone."

was summoned by the emperor to become editorial director, but he didn't take up the post. He then wrote a letter to Yue and the others, saying, "Names are guests of realities, something I've never wanted. With no heart in the center, it's vain to work for south or north. Contrived benevolence is on the contrary criminal; I will remain right here."

When he was more than eighty years old he was still writing commentaries, in fine script under a lamp. Altogether these amounted to two or three thousand scrolls. People of the time considered this a product of calm silence for taking care of the body.

He composed "Black Butterfly Elegies" to convey his ideas. He annotated both appendixes to the *I Ching,* the inner chapters of *Chuang-tzu, Essentials of Lao-tzu,* and wrote several dozen volumes on other classics.

He died at home in his eighty-fifth year. His final instructions as he was dying were based on Huangfu Xuanyan.[19] A copy of *The Classic of Filial Piety* was deposited in his casket.

The casket was placed in a shallow grave, and no place for offerings was set up. He used to set out water as an offering to spirits every season, and his son Yi carried out this practice in his honor.

Lu Huixiao[20] and Zhang Rong[21] of Wujun both composed obituaries for him. The Tang dynasty inspector Yan Zhenqing composed *Record of Virtues of the Exemplars of the Shen Clan* to express appreciation and set up an ancestral tablet to honor his excellence. His grave is on Golden Goose Mountain.

Taoist Disposition

Yu Yi

Yu Yi was styled Yaojian. He was a man of Xinye.[22] His natural inclination was toward calm and quiet, not to interact with external things.

---

19. That is, Huangfu Mi.
20. This man also appears in Buddhist annals, as a lay patron of a distinguished monk named Sengna. Cf. *Gaosengchuan erji* 6.
21. Zhang Rong (444–497) held a number of posts under the (Liu) Song and (Southern) Qi dynasties and was also a writer of some distinction.
22. In Henan.

When the king of Linquan visited his province, a memorial recommending him was submitted, and the king sent him a gift of one thousand pecks of wheat. He stoutly refused, saying to the envoy, "I am a companion of woodcutters and wild deer and will wear coarse wool all of my life. Racing the chariot of the sun and moon, guaranteeing my income by tilling the soil myself, I am already deeply indebted to the great king."

He enjoyed himself with literary gatherings. The administrator of Anxi, Yuan Tuan, admired his ways and gave him gifts of a staghorn arm support for writing, a mother-of-pearl inkstone, and an ivory brush. He also presented a verse saying:

> The bright sun shines clearly,
> The blue sky quietly lights up.
> We've heard of Chao and Xu[23] of old;
> Now I see antiquity.

Yi reciprocated with a woven-bamboo arm support for writing.

In 496 he was officially summoned to serve as recorder for the Minister of Works, but he didn't take up the office. Then he died.

Taoist Scholarship

YU CHENGXIAN

Yu Chengxian was styled Zitong. He was a man of Yanling in Yingchuan.[24] Habitually quiet, he had will. Right and wrong were never involved in his words, joy and anger never appeared on his face. No one could see into him.

He comprehended all the mystic scriptures and esoteric classics. He thoroughly studied all currents of thought and all categories of literature. Then he traveled to Mount Heng with the Taoist priest Wang Sengzhen.

The Loyal Righteous King of Poyang[25] admired his character and wanted to spend time with him. He had him lecture on Lao-tzu, and

23. That is, Chao Fu and Xu You, legendary free men of predynastic times. When Chao Fu was offered the throne, he washed out his ears; when Xu You heard of this, he led his ox upstream to drink.
24. In Henan.
25. In Guangxi.

famous gentlemen from far and near all came to the gatherings. When debates arose, Chengxian replied serenely, and everyone learned something new.

In 531 Liu Huifei[26] of Mount Lu came to Jingzhou. Chengxian had known him from long before, so he went to follow him. Students from Jingzhou and Shaanxi took the opportunity to request Chengxian to lecture on Lao-tzu, and the king of Xiangdong came to listen. After Chengxian returned to the mountain, the king personally began to follow the Way and also sent a gift of a collection of poetry.

Taoist Character

TAO HONGJING

Tao Hongjing was styled Tongming. He was a man of Moling.[27] When he was ten years old he got Ge Hong's *Stories of Spiritual Immortals* and read it. He told people, "Gazing up at the blue clouds, I saw the white sun, and it didn't seem to be distant." His spirit and conduct were intelligent and outstanding. His eyes were bright, his eyebrows separate; he was thin, with a long forehead and protruding ears. On his right knee were several dozen black spots forming a pattern of seven stars.

He read more than ten thousand scrolls and considered it a profound disgrace if there were a single thing he didn't know. He was good at the lute and chess and skilled at cursive and square calligraphy. Before he reached his majority, [future] emperor Gao of the Qi dynasty [r. 479–483], then acting as prime minister, took him on as an attendant reader and got many of his precedents for court appointments and invitations of scholars from him.

His family was poor, and when he sought to govern the district he didn't succeed. In 492 he took off his court costume, hung it up on the gate of the spiritual warrior, and submitted his resignation to the em-

26. Liu Huifei was a gentleman who retired from civil service to become a recluse. Known as the Purified Professor, he was also interested in Buddhism and lived at the Eastern Forest Temple on Mount Lu, the first Pure Land Buddhist center in China. According to Buddhist annals, he was skilled at the seal and clerical scripts and copied more than two thousand scrolls of Buddhist scripture in his own hand, a traditional concentration practice.

27. An old name of Nanjing, in Jiangsu, capital of several dynasties mentioned hitherto in the stories, including the Jin, Liu Song, Qi, and Liang dynasties.

peror, who issued a statement accepting it. He was given a bolt of white silk and an imperial decree providing that he receive a monthly supply of five pounds of poria[28] and two pints of honey for his diet, wherever he might be. When he departed, nobles followed him to Zhenglu station. They all said, "Since the Song and Qi dynasties there has never been such a thing."

Now he stopped at Juqu Mountain [Maoshan] in Jurong. He built a lodge in the mountains and called himself the Recluse of Huayang.[29] In his correspondence with people he substituted "the Recluse" for his name.

First he received talismans, diagrams, and scriptural teachings from Sun Youyue of Dongyang, traveled to all the famous mountains left of the river, and sought out traces of the realized ones Yang Xi and the Xus [Xu Mai, Xu Mu, and Xu Hui].[30]

He once told his disciples, "I saw the great mansions of aristocrats, and though I recognized their glory, I had no desire to go. Gazing up at lofty mountains, looking down on vast wilds, while realizing it is hard to be established here, this is just where I've always wanted to go. During the Yongming era [483–494] I sought official ranks and got diverted right away. Had that not happened, how could I be doing what I do today?"

The maestro had a well-rounded personality, deferential and respectful, unobtrusively blending in wherever he went. His mind was like a clear mirror, immediately understanding whatever he encountered. There was no confusion or contradiction in his words, and they also had enlightening aftereffects.

In the beginning of the Yongyuan era [499–501], he also built a three-story building. Disciples and guests stayed below, while he cut himself off from people.

He was especially fond of the wind in the pines and enjoyed hearing that sound. Sometimes he'd wander alone to springs and mountaintops, and those who saw him from a distance thought he was an

28. *Poria cocos* (hoelen), colloquially called Indian bread in English, is *fuling* in Chinese. It is said to have diuretic, sedative, anti-inflammatory, antitumor, immunological, and antiemetic effects.

29. Huayang is a name for the eighth great grotto heaven of Maoshan.

30. Tao compiled and annotated *Declarations of the Realized* based on the revelations of these mystics. Because of his role in the organization of the materials, Tao is sometimes considered the de facto founder of the Maoshan cult.

immortal. He was naturally fond of writing and valued the extraordinary. He was particularly well versed in yin-yang and the five elements; wind divination; star calculation; topography of mountains, rivers, and land; mapping of local products; medical arts and herbs; and the reigns and dates of emperors and dynasties. He constructed an astrolabe three feet high, with the earth in the center; the sky turned while the earth stood still. It was run mechanically in complete accord with the natural sky. He said it was necessary for practicing the Way.

He deeply admired the character of Zhang Liang, saying that none of the savants of old could compare to him. At the end of the Qi dynasty he made a prediction, "[Characters meaning] *water cutting wood* [combined] make [the character] *Liang.*"[31] Then when the army of Wu of Liang[32] reached Xincheng, Tao sent his disciple Dai Mengzhi to make his way through alien territory to convey a message to the emperor. Then when he heard there was discussion of abdication, the maestro drew diagrammatic prognoses according to several methods, and all of them came up *Liang.* So he had a disciple present this.

Since the [new] emperor had already spent time with him early on, once he assumed the throne his generosity and courtesies became even more earnest. The maestro had already gotten the secret of miraculous talismans; time and again he made miraculous elixir and stopped. The emperor always provided him with medicinal substances. He even took a flying elixir Tao prepared, and it had effect, increasing the emperor's respect for the maestro. When the emperor had books presented to him, he lit incense and received them reverently.

The emperor had Tao compose a cycle of years. When he came to

31. This is a simple example of one elementary method of encryption, but it is enough to illustrate the essential reason that literary Chinese cannot be translated by machine.

32. Emperor Wu, founder of the Liang dynasty, reigned for an exceptionally long time, from 502 to 550, but his reputation in history is blemished, not least by the rebellion of his general Hou Jing in 548. In Buddhist lore Wu is portrayed as having an Ashoka complex, imagining himself like the ancient Indian emperor, in the sense of lavishly patronizing Buddhism in order to cleanse his conscience of the blood he had shed in the process of establishing his dominion. Wu is criticized for trying to practice generosity by economically ruinous donations to monasteries and for trying to practice compassion by forgiving corrupt officials in his organization. In Chan Buddhist lore he is portrayed as a superficialist without any actual enlightenment. See *The Blue Cliff Record* by Thomas Cleary and J. C. Cleary (1977, 1992), case 1.

the 6/6 year, he affixed a crimson dot. It turned out to be the third year of the Taiqing era of the Liang dynasty.[33]

The emperor personally summoned him and presented him with a deerskin turban. He just drew two oxen in reply; one ox was roaming freely between water and grassland, and one had gold encasing its head, with a man holding it by a rope and driving it with a stick. The emperor laughed and said, "There's nothing this man doesn't do, but he wants to emulate the turtle dragging its tail. How could he be induced in any way!" In important matters of state, he always consulted the maestro first; every month there were always several messages. People of the time called Tao the Prime Minister in the Mountains.

In 504 he moved to the valley east of Piled Gold Peak of Maoshan in order to practice the higher path. He remained secluding himself for forty-some years. When he was more than eighty he had the appearance of a man in his prime.

A book of immortals says, "Those with square eyes live a thousand years." In the maestro's last years, one of his eyes was sometimes square.

As he had a subtle understanding of technical calculations, he knew in advance that the fortunes of the Liang dynasty were going to reverse. He composed a poem beforehand that said:

> Wang Yan gave vent to idle nonsense,
> He Yan sat discussing emptiness.[34]
> How could they answer to the Mansion of the Shining Sun's[35]
> Being turned into the palace of a Hunnish chief?[36]

33. This was to be the last year of the reign and life of the emperor.

34. Wang Yan (256–311) served the Jin dynasty as minister of education. He was killed by Shi Lu, founder of the Later Zhao dynasty, which drove the Jin out of northern China. He Yan (190–249) served as palace attendant and imperial secretary for the kingdom of Wei during the era of the Three Kingdoms. He Yan was killed by Sima Yi (179–251), a Jin general and politician whose grandson founded the Jin dynasty. Both He Yan and Wang Yan were devotees of the philosophical stream known as *qingtan*, or pure conversation, often criticized as excessively abstract.

35. The name of a palace, originally built by Emperor Cheng of the Han dynasty (r. 31–7 B.C.E.).

36. Shi Lu, who killed Wang Yan and drove the "native" Jin dynasty out of northern China, was ethnically a Jie, people related to the Xiongnu, or Huns, who had been the main adversaries of the Han dynasty.

He hid this poem in a box; his disciples found it only after his death. Now, at the end of the Datong era of Liang [535–546], the gentry vied in discussion of mysticism and didn't practice military service. Then when Hou Jing usurped the throne, after all it was in the Mansion of the Shining Sun!

The maestro already knew beforehand when he was going to die and composed "Announcement of Departure." He died in 536, at the age of eighty-one. He was given the title of court gentleman and was posthumously named Maestro of Moral Purity. *The Mountain World Book* he wrote comprised several hundred scrolls, and disciples who received his teachings numbered more than three thousand.

His nephew Xu compiled *Biography of Maestro Tao, Recluse of Huayang.* Xie Lun[37] of Wuxing compiled *A Brief Account of Maestro Tao.* Li Po compiled *The Story of the Liang Dynasty Maestro of Moral Purity of Maoshan,*[38] Gu Song[39] compiled *The Inside Story of Realized Man Tao, Overseer of Waters on Penglai.* The Xuanhe emperor [of the Song dynasty, Huizong, r. 1101–1126] decreed him Realized Man Assisting Education as Religious Chief.

The imperial decree stated, "Having received the revered mandate of the nephrite heavens, we hold the precious talisman of imperial China. Now then, we are going to broadcast a note of spirituality to expand respect for the influence of the Way, publicize subtle statements about the supreme teaching, and promote a good name to the ranks of the realized. Tao the Recluse, Overseer of Waters of Penglai, had a history of praiseworthy conduct, purifying the imperial palace. He communicated spiritually without imposition or involvement; though he manifestly ministered in the mountains, with his accurate intuition and foresight it was granted he'd already attained immortality at sea. Considering his incomparable repute, how dare we forget his occult protection? May the glory of an honorable, beautiful title of distinction forever mediate blessings to benefit the living."

ZHOU ZILIANG

Zhou Ziliang was styled Yuanhe. He was a disciple of Tao the Recluse of Maoshan. He was originally a man of Runan prefecture in

---

37. Xie Lun appears in *The Golden Broth of Buddhism,* vol. 4, as a friend of the distinguished recluse He Dian.
38. Cf. *Yunji qiqian,* in *Daozang jiyao,* vol. 19, pp. 8430b–31b.
39. A Tang dynasty poet.

Yuzhou,[40] but he resided in Qinhua Village in the western district of Jiankang in Danyang.[41] His grandfather Wenliang had been a court attendant of the principality of Jiangxia during the Song dynasty. His biological father, Yaozong, the fifth son of Wenliang, administrator of the five offices of the county, died early. His uncle Yaoxu, his adoptive father, was on the staff of the Ministry of Rites in Yangzhou.[42]

His mother was Xu Jingguang of Yongjia.[43] When she was five months pregnant, she dreamed that immortals and sages appeared in her room, encircling her.

Zhou Ziliang was born on the second day of the first month of 495, at the hour when people settle down. In his tenth year, he accompanied his mother to Yongjia. In 508, when the Recluse [Tao Hongjing] was traveling to the sea and mountains in the east, he crossed the mountain road into Yongjia, where he put up at the Celestial Teacher's Lodge. Now, Ziliang was already staying there; he was twelve years old at the time. He took the opportunity to seek to go into the mountains, take up discipline, and become a disciple. First he received miraculous omens of immortals, the five-thousand-character writing of Lao-tzu, and the talisman of the Lord of West Mountain[44] for warding off tigers and leopards. Then he concentrated on attending to incense and lamps.

He was generally fond of calligraphy and painting. He was able to perform the various arts people practice as soon as he was exposed to them. Later he went along to Nanhuo, then back to Muliu.[45] In 512 he followed Tao back to Maoshan, where he went on to receive maps of the five sacred mountains and the *Inner Writings of the Three August Ones*.[46]

In the autumn of 513 his family announced that his relatives were going to come to live in the mountains. He went off to stay in a separate lodge in the west hills.

Ziliang secretly received spiritual teachings, inducing realized people to descend and contacting immortals. The Recluse never once had

40. In Henan.
41. In Jiangsu.
42. In Jiangsu.
43. In Zhejiang.
44. West Mountain is the name of the twelfth of the thirty-six minor grotto heavens of Taoism, governed by the realized man Tang Gongcheng.
45. In Yongjia.
46. See the story of Bao Jing.

any doubt about this. It seems that on the twenty-third day of the fifth month, the first day of the summer of 513, he suddenly lay down, then after a while got up; this was the beginning of the induced descents. On the twenty-seventh day of the tenth month, after the sun had set, he lay down flat and left his body. He was twenty years old at the time.

The Recluse disposed of his effects and found no records left, for all time. The following month, however, when he went to the Yankou cave, he did find a big box of writings. So then he climbed a steep mountain and took them out. Prostrating himself and praying to be allowed to take them back, he found them to be messages that Ziliang had been receiving. The writings sealed in the box were on loose sheets, all scrambled, so he ordered them by date, arranging them into *Records of Mr. Zhou's Communications with the Unseen* in four scrolls. The Recluse also wrote *The Story of Zhou, Man of Mystery* as a preface to the *Records*. He presented this to Emperor Wu [of Liang].

Ziliang studied the Way for three lifetimes altogether.[47] First he was born into the family of Zhou Da; next he was born into the family of Liu Wei. The blessings of his diligence in studying the Way were only realized in his present incarnation. He had already been entered in the registry of immortals three times; in that interval he may have committed offenses that resulted in repeated descent, so it was only after going through birth and death that he finally succeeded in gaining access to the Office of Preserving Life. Changing his name to Taixuan, styled Xuling, he became chief keeper of the registry. Later he petitioned Donghua[48] to become keeper of the dawn, and his name was engraved on a purple jade slip. Many realized ones came down to teach him mystic doctrines, as detailed in the aforementioned records.

47. This Buddhistic conception is ostensibly used to explain why this individual died so young, but the immediate cause of premature death may have been connected to the strain of the practices of Taoist mediums and the neurological states they induce or to which they are subject. Xu Hui, who also experienced psychic visitations, likewise died at the early age of thirty. Yang Xi, who also had these experiences, only lived to be fifty-seven, no great age for a Taoist.

48. A center of esoteric Taoist government, also shorthand for the name of a supernal Taoist authority.

Taoist Arts

SUN WENTAO

Sun Wentao, also named Tao, was styled Wenzang. He was a man of Yan prefecture in Huiji. He entered Maoshan and took the Recluse for his teacher, studying and learning methods of realization. He even saw the supreme scriptures written by the three realized ones, Yang [Xi] and the three Xus [Xu Mai, Xu Mu, and Xu Hui], in their own handwriting. With a little practice copying, he turned out to be very skillful.

Later he copied the calligraphy of Wang Xizhi and had a particularly profound attainment. Contemporaries praised him for an inscription on the tablet of the south cave of Huayang. The altar tablets in administrator Xu's old office are all Tao's calligraphy. The reverse side of the tablet of the south cave says, "Wentao's heart was soft while his countenance was firm; his conduct was straight while his wisdom was round. Since his work was exceptional, his unusual writings were engraved." Regarding the engraving of unusual writings mentioned, there is no information anymore in the mountains.

A Taoist Scholar

MA SHU

Ma Shu, styled Yaoli, was a man of Mei in Fufeng.[49] He was widely learned in the classics and histories, particularly expert in the doctrines of the *I Ching* and *Lao-tzu*. When Liu, king of Shaoling, was inspector of southern Xu province,[50] he recruited Ma to be an academic. When Hou Jing started a civil war, Liu raised an army to help the emperor; at that time he entrusted twenty thousand scrolls of writings to Shu. Shu decided to read through them and was nearly finished when he sighed, "I've heard that those who value rank and status consider Chao Fu and Xu You[51] to have been fettered, while those who like

---

49. In Shaanxi.
50. In Jiangsu.
51. Chao Fu and Xu You refused to have anything to do with politics, so it is said that their example is repudiated by those with worldly ambitions.

mountains and forests consider Yi and Lu[52] to have been warehouse keepers. To get bound up in name and fact trashes the loftiness of Lao-tzu; to enjoy purity and emptiness is to trivialize the doctrines of Confucius. In serious discourse comparing them, still each follows his preference. Recently men who seek their aim look up the road and stop. How could it be that heaven does not favor loftiness? Why is so little heard of the mountains and forests?" So then he went into seclusion on Maoshan, determined to spend the rest of his life there.

Shu's family was scattered by civil war when he was young. Wherever he lived, robbers and bandits did not invade, so there were always several hundred families depending on him. In the first year of the Tianxi era [560] of the Chen dynasty, Emperor Wen summoned Ma to become minister of revenue, but he refused and did not obey the order.

In his late years, his eyeballs became hollow and yellow, and he could see things in the dark. A pair of white swallows nested in a tree in his yard; they frequented his railings and eaves, sometimes even coming to his desk, arriving in spring and leaving in autumn for nearly thirty years.

He died in 581. He wrote *Treatise on the Way and Consciousness*, which circulated in the world.

Taoist Character

XUE BIAOZHI

Xue Biaozhi was a man of Jinling.[53] From youth he did not take to convention and had no craving for glory and status. In 495 he lodged in Dongchuan,[54] searching for the secrets of realization; he came back after three years. He began to practice Taoism in a cave chamber of Maoshan, eating pine nuts and drinking from streams for years on

52. Yi and Lu were two of the famous Four Elders. They got involved with the imperial house, so it is said that their example is repudiated by recluses.

53. Jinling is an old name of Nanjing, capital of several southern dynasties, in Jiangsu, where Maoshan is located.

54. In Yunnan.

end. This chamber was where the realized man Ren Dun[55] of the Jin dynasty had attained the Way; his altar and stove were still there and had distinct miraculous effects. This is why the maestro went there in quest of the ancient, to seek realization.

55. Ren Dun studied Taoism on Mount Luofu, then later lived in the southern grotto of Maoshan, where he had many disciples. He was supposedly able to command ghosts and spirits, to appear in multiple forms, and to be invulnerable to wild beasts.

[8]

SUI DYNASTY
(589–618) and

TANG DYNASTY
(618–906)

Taoist Character

WANG YUANZHI

Wang Yuanzhi was a man of Langye.[1] His grandfather Jingxuan had been inspector of Jiangzhou during the Liang dynasty; his father Tanxuan was inspector of Yangzhou under the Chen dynasty. His mother was a daughter of Ding Chao, gentleman of the interior of the Ministry of War. Once when she was napping in the daytime, she dreamed miraculous phoenixes gathered about her. Then it turned out she was pregnant. Also, she heard the sound of crying in her belly.

The *True Record of Monks*[2] says, "Tanxuan was a child produced during the day; he will be a chamberlain for the imperial clan of spiritual immortals."

Yuanzhi was born in 528. He was bright and quick to learn in youth and was widely read. His first teacher was Maestro Zongdao, Zang Jing;[3] later he went into Maoshan, where he inherited and applied Recluse Tao's scriptural teachings.

---

1. In Shandong.
2. *Shamen shizhi*. No such text seems to be extant. At a glance, *shizhi* looks like a misprint for *baozhi*, in which case the title would yield the name of the notorious Buddhist monk (*shamen*) Baozhi, who appeared at the court of Emperor Wu of Liang and whose standard profile would fit the image portrayed here of a soothsayer. Baozhi is supposed to have died before Tanxuan was born, but he was also famous for foretelling future events accurately. Cf. *Jingdechuandenglu* 27, and *The Blue Cliff Record*, cases 1 and 67.
3. Zang Jing was a contemporary leader of the Maoshan sect.

The emperor of Chen, hearing of his repute, invited, him into the Double Yang Palace to lecture, and he was showered with praise. Then when the future emperor Yang of the Sui dynasty was king of Jin occupying Yangzhou, he had Wang Zixiang and Liu Guyan invite Yuanzhi, one after the other, so he then came for an audience. His hair immediately became white, and the emperor got scared and sent him away. After a while he reverted to his former appearance.

When Emperor Yang visited Zhuojun, Supernumerary Vice-Minister Cui Feng recommended Yuanzhi, so the emperor went to greet him, meeting at Linshuo Palace. The emperor personally enrolled as his disciple and ordered the capital city to construct Jade Purity Mystic Altar to house Yuanzhi. Then when the emperor visited Yangzhou, Yuanzhi counseled him not to go far from the capital, but the emperor was unable to comply.

Before Emperor Gaozu [r. 618–627] founded the Tang dynasty, Yuanzhi had secretly transmitted the divine decree. During the Wude era [618–627], the future emperor Taizong, putting down Wang Shichong,[4] went with [his adviser] Fang Xuanling in plain clothes to call on Yuanzhi. Greeting them, Yuanzhi said, "One of you is a ruler; is it not the king of Qin?" Taizong, who was then king of Qin, therefore told him the truth. Yuanzhi said, "You're going to be an emperor over great peace; please take care of yourself." When Taizong assumed the imperial throne, he was going to confer a high rank on him, but Yuanzhi insisted on going back to the mountains.

In 635 the emperor commanded Run province to establish Great Peace Monastery on Maoshan and to ordain Taoist priests. The document that came down bearing the imperial seal said, "The maestro's disciplined conduct is plain and simple, his virtuous action is harmonious and pure. Shutting out the confusion of the material world, he sets his will on mystic emptiness. Exhaling the old and inhaling the new, he consumes fungus and eats atractylodes. Minding myriad marvels beyond the Three Purities, he caused white hair to reverse after the age of one hundred. His way transcends precedents, his reputation is the loftiest since antiquity. Without having obtained secret instructions at an altar of gold and received mystic writings from a book-pack of jade, who could be equal to this?

---

4. Wang Shichong (d. 621) was a general of the Sui dynasty who deposed the last emperor of Sui and tried to establish his own supremacy. In the process he also defeated Li Mi, another general who rebelled against the Sui dynasty.

"In the past, when we were in a regional court, we already got to ask about the Way; we never forgot the well-considered words and circumspect guidelines, whether waking or sleeping. Recently we read an incoming memorial requesting permission to return to the mountain where he used to stay, but we already have a different directive, which does not overlook his lofty aim and also allows for establishment of a monastery, to show our long-standing aspiration. We do not know when the maestro will arrive; when will the buildings being constructed beyond the river be done? We are waiting to hear the details, according to these expectations. Recently we have already sent the grand astrologer Xue Yi and others to go visit, directing him to set forth our wish."

On the fourteenth day of the eighth lunar month of that year, Yuanzhi said to his disciple Pan Shizheng, "I have been evaluated for immortality and cannot ascend to heaven in broad daylight by myself because I mistakenly hurt a boy's lips when I was a child. I am registered as the Earl of Few Houses Mountain, and I am going there to take up the post." On the sixteenth he bathed, donned his hat and robe, lit incense, and lay down. Turning to an attendant, he asked, "What time is it?" The attendant replied that it was the hour of the dragon [7:00 to 9:00 A.M.]. He said, "Good," then straightened his hat and passed on. He was 126 years old.

In 670, he was given the title Superior Grand Master of the Palace and the posthumous name Maestro Ascended to Reality. The empress Zetian[5] bestowed the additional title of Imperial Aide of the Gold and Violet Order.[6] In 691 she changed his posthumous name to Maestro Ascended to the Mysterious. In his time he was called Religious Leader Wang.

Taoist Advice

XU HONGKE

Xu Hongke was a Taoist priest of Mount Tai. When the Sui dynasty was in disarray, he wrote a letter to Li Mi[7] saying, "When a large mass

5. Lived from 625 to 705. The dates of her reign are accounted variously, as she took over administrative authority some time before formally declaring a new dynasty under her supreme rule in 690. She was also a devotee and patron of Buddhism.

6. The combination of gold and violet is emblematic of the highest order of court rank, above the silver and blue order mentioned in an earlier story.

7. Li Mi was a general and chief strategist of a rebellion against the ruling house of the Sui dynasty.

of people have been gathered together for a long time, there is the fear that the rice will run out, the people will drift away, the advisers and elders will become tired of war, and it will be hard to succeed. It is opportune to take advantage of the chance to advance and take over, issuing the best of your warriors and horses, following the current to the east, heading right for Jiangdou to seize the isolated man[8] and command the whole land."

Mi was impressed by his advice and sent a letter inviting him. But Hongke never emerged, and no one knew where he went.

Master Hu of Zhitang said, "Hongke's strategy was extraordinary but correct; not only was Li Mi not his equal, none of the men of Tang were his equal. It's not that the world ever lacks talented people, but some conceal themselves in butcher shops or lodge among rebels. Hongke and Wei Cheng[9] sojourned among the Taoist clergy yet cherished plans to rectify the times, concerned with means of saving the world, yet nobody knew. Emperor Yang of Sui [r. 605–616] was unprincipled, so the resentment of the people was due, the rebellion of the military was due, the alienation of the aristocracy was due.

"To be a Taoist priest one resides in the haze and mist, sheds traces of dust and dirt; as for the successes and failures of human rulers, the order and chaos of society, why is that one's concern? And yet he spoke out in his indignation, profoundly understanding essentials, urging men to settle their strategy and directly arrest the isolated man. The *Classic of Poetry* says, 'People's constancy to morality is beautiful character indeed.' This is what it means!

"But Li Mi was not worth talking to. Hongke could not but have known that Li Shimin[10] had raised an army, but he may have had no way to reach him on his own, so he relied on Li Mi to reveal this. By this one piece of advice you can see how there was certainly much that was extraordinary in this man's heart, and yet he didn't show off. Even when to-be emperor Taizong [that is, Li Shimin] had taken over the

8. *Isolated man* is a Confucian technical term for a ruler who has lost his mandate through inhumanity to his subjects. The principle is that such a person is no longer a sacrosanct son of heaven but an individual isolated man against whom measures may legitimately be taken for his injustices. This conception of legitimate revolution is represented in *Mencius*.

9. Wei Cheng is the subject of the next story.

10. Li Shimin (599–649), a much celebrated figure in Chinese history, was to become cofounder and second emperor of the Tang dynasty.

land, there was still no word of him—had he already died? Was he like Huangshigong[11] or Lu Zhonglian?[12] Ah! He can be called a lofty man!"

Taoism and Authority

WEI CHENG

Wei Cheng was styled Xuancheng. He was a man of Qucheng in Weizhou.[13] Orphaned when young, losing his prospects, he abandoned his property and didn't manage it, having greater aims.

When the Sui dynasty was in chaos, he went into seclusion and became a Taoist priest. Later he assisted Emperor Taizong [of the Tang dynasty], urging him by direct counsel to practice humaneness and justice, bringing about the great peace of the Zhengguan era [627–650], becoming the first-generation religious minister.

The biography in the *Book of Han* does not give the complete record.

Taoist Arts

XU ZE

Xu Ze was a man of Yan on the Eastern Sea.[14] As a boy he was given to silence and had few desires. He received instruction from Zhou

11. Huangshigong, "Mr. Yellowstone," was the legendary mentor of the patriot Zhang Liang, who, like Lu Zhonglian, opposed the militant Qin.

12. Lu Zhonglian was a learned man of the Warring States era. According to the account in *Shiji*, he wouldn't work in government but had a penchant for solving people's problems. A native of the ancient state of Qi, he was on a trip to the state of Zhao when the latter was besieged by the armies of the powerful state of Qin, which would eventually consolidate the ancient states into an empire. Meanwhile, the state of Wei sent an army to Zhao to reinforce Zhao against Qin. The Wei general, however, advocated submission to the authority of Qin. Lu Zhonglian, though an outsider, stepped in and refused submission on behalf of the ruler of Zhao, as a matter of principle. Then the Qin army was driven out and Zhao was rescued. As a traditional didactic tale, the story represents precedence of principle over personal interest. When the lord of Zhao tried to reward Lu Zhonglian, he is reported to have said, "What is valued by knights all over the world is to get rid of troubles, relieve hardships, and resolve confusion and disorder for people, not to take. To be a taker is the business of a merchant, not something I can bear to do." Then he left and was never seen again.

13. In Shandong.

14. Yan was in Zhejiang; here Donghai, "Eastern Sea," is used as a general term for the eastern seaboard rather than a specific term for the region by that name comprising parts of Shandong and Jiangsu.

Hongzheng.[15] He mastered the three mystic texts[16] and was expert at debate. His fame resounded in the capital. Ze lamented, "A name is a guest of reality; should I be a guest?" So he subsequently took the discipline of seclusion to heart and hiked into Pink Cloud Mountain.[17] Several hundred people went along to study from him.

During the Taijian era [569–582] of the Chen dynasty, he complied with an imperial order to come to stay at the Taoist monastery Perfect Reality. After a month he took leave and went into Mount Tiantai, where he stopped eating grain and cultivated nature, living on nothing but pine nuts and atractylodes. Even in the freezing cold of the dead of winter he didn't wear padded clothing.

When he was first on Pink Cloud Mountain, the Realized Man of the Absolute, Master Xu,[18] descended and said to him, "When you're more than eighty years old you'll be a teacher of royalty; after that you'll attain the Way." At that time Guang, king of Jin,[19] was occupying Yangzhou; he heard of Ze's reputation and personally wrote a letter inviting him. Ze said to his disciples, "I'm eighty-one this year, and a king has come inviting me. Master Xu's words have proven true!" So he went to the king.

The king asked to receive Taoist teachings, but Ze refused on the grounds that the time was not convenient. Afterward, in the middle of the night he told attendants to hold incense burners, as in an ordinary morning ritual; during the fifth watch [3:00 to 5:00 A.M.] he died.

His limbs and body were flexible and soft as in life; he remained there for weeks with no change in the color of his face. The king sent an envoy to return him to Tiantai to be entombed.

At that time, many people on the road all the way from Jiangdou to Tiantai saw Ze walking on foot, saying he'd been freed to return. When

---

15. A brilliant scholar of the Chen dynasty, said to have mastered the *Tao Te Ching* and the *I Ching* when he was ten years old and to have become a university student at the age of fifteen. He eventually became senior officer of the Imperial Secretariat. He wrote commentaries on *Lao-tzu*, Confucius, *Chuang-tzu*, and the *Classic of Filial Piety.*

16. *Lao-tzu, Chuang-tzu,* and *I Ching.*

17. In Zhejiang.

18. Xu Lailu. He is mentioned in *Lingbao lueji* in *Yunji qiqian,* described as having been commissioned by a supernal sage to teach Taoist scriptures. Cf. *Daozang jiyao,* vol. 19, p. 8417a.

19. Crown prince of the Sui dynasty.

he reached his former abode, he distributed his scriptures and writings and implements among his disciples. Then he had a room cleaned, saying, "There will be a guest arriving; he should be received." Then he crossed the stone bridge and left, no one knew where.

A moment later the casket arrived, and then they realized he'd turned into a spirit. He was eighty-two years old at the time.

When the king heard about this, he marveled at him all the more and sent a painter to make a portrait of him. Liu Bian[20] wrote a eulogy for this.

XUE YI

Xue Yi was a man of Fenyin,[21] east of the Yellow River. When he was young he took a liking to mystic sayings; during the Daye era [of the Sui dynasty, 605–616] he left ordinary society to become a Taoist priest. He understood astronomy and calendography. In the time of Emperor Yang [of the Sui dynasty, r. 605–616] he was brought into the inner sanctuary of the Jade Purity Monastery and soon made to lead prayers. In the beginning of the Wude era [of the Tang dynasty, 618–627] he was sent to Qin prefecture. Yi had once privately said to the king of Qin [Li Shimin, future cofounder and emperor of the Tang dynasty], "The star of virtue protects the lot of Qin; Your Majesty will rule the whole land. Please take care of yourself." After a series of transfers, he reached the rank of chief astrologer.

During the Zhengguan era [of the Tang dynasty, 627–650], the emperor was going to perform sacrifices to heaven and earth on Mount Tai, but a comet appeared, and so Yi told him he'd considered various esoteric signs and it might not be appropriate to sacrifice to the east. As it happened, Chu Suiliang[22] also spoke of this matter, and so the emperor gave up the idea.

Later Yi petitioned the emperor to allow him to become a Taoist priest again. Emperor Taizong set up a monastery for him and appointed him grand master to carry out the direction of the monastery affairs. The emperor also ordered an observatory to be set up in the

20. Liu Bian served the second emperor of the Sui dynasty as supervisor of the Palace Secretariat.
21. In Shandong.
22. Chu Suiliang (597–658) was chancellor under the first two emperors of the Tang dynasty.

monastery, to observe occult signs; whenever there were bad or good omens, eclipses, or strange atmospheric conditions, Yi reported them to the emperor. Many of his reports coincided with those of Li Chun-feng[23] in the observatory in the capital city. Chunfeng had also been a Taoist priest during the Sui dynasty, called Professor Yellow Hat, distinguishing himself through discourse and writings.

A Taoist Recluse

WANG JI

Wang Ji was styled Wugong. He was a man of Longmen in Ganzhou.[24] He was simple and free by nature, not fond of bowing and saluting. His elder brother Tong was a great scholar of the late Sui dynasty. Ji repeatedly responded to recommendations for *filial piety and brotherliness* and *uncorrupted integrity* and was given the post of proofreader in the imperial library. He didn't like it and sought to become chief of Linhe.[25] Because he was addicted to wine, he didn't do his job. At the time, the whole land was in chaos, so he quit and left. He lamented, "The all-encompassing net is in the heavens; where shall I go?" Then he returned to his native village, where he had about 240 acres of fields on a river islet.

There was a recluse, Zhongchang Ziguang, who consumed a special diet for health; Ji admired his genuine simplicity and moved nearby. Ziguang was mute and never conversed. They once had a drink together and quietly had a good time.

Ji had several servants who planted millet, made wine in spring and autumn, raised ducks and geese, and planted medicinal herbs, providing for self-support. He kept the *I Ching, Lao-tzu,* and *Chuang-tzu* at the head of his bed and rarely read other books. When he wanted to see his brother, he'd cross the river and go back home.

He loved to wander in the mountains to the north, Donggao, so he was called the Scholar of Donggao. Riding an ox through the wine market, he'd stay for several days. In the beginning of the Wude era [of the Tang dynasty, 618–627], because his earlier office had been in the chan-

23. Li Chunfeng was a distinguished astronomer, mathematician, and calendarist.
24. In Shanxi.
25. In Jiangsu.

cellery of officials attendant upon imperial command, he was given an official allowance of three liters of wine per day. Someone asked, "What's the pleasure in being attendant upon imperial command?" He replied, "Fine brewed wine is enjoyable, that's all." He died in 644.

Taoist Character

SHE FANSHAN

She Fashan was a man of Guacang.[26] Three generations from his great-grandfather became Taoist priests; all of them transmitted arts of divination and health maintenance. He received talismans in youth and was able to arrest ghosts and spirits.

During the Xianqing era [of the Tang dynasty, 650–656], Emperor Gaozong heard of him and ordered him to the capital city. The emperor was going to confer title and rank on him, but he stoutly refused them. He was kept in an inner sanctuary, where he was given special treatment.

At that time Emperor Gaozong was recruiting magicians from all over to collaborate on material alchemy. Fashan advised the emperor, "Gold elixir is hard to make; it wastes resources and occasions lapses in government administration. Please distinguish the true from the false." The emperor agreed with what he said and consequently had Fashan test the magicians; more than ninety people came forth, and he dismissed them all.

Over a period of fifty years, from the reign of Gaozong [650–684] to Zetian [684–705] and Zhongzong [705–710], Fashan was always traveling around to famous mountains; he was invited into the imperial palace numerous times and was questioned about the Way with all courtesy. When Ruizong assumed the throne [in 710], he praised Fashan's achievement in occult assistance. In 713 Fashan was appointed chief of the Office of Foreign Affairs and enfeoffed as duke of the state of Yue. But he continued to be a Taoist priest as before and resided in Jinglong Monastery in the capital city. His father, Huiming, was given an honorific court gentleman title, and the inspector of Shezhou, Li Yong, composed a memorial inscription. The imperial favor he received in that time was without compare.

26. In Zhejiang. Mount Guacang contains the tenth of the Ten Great Grotto Heavens of Taoism.

Fashan was born in 614 and died in 720, around the age of 107. An imperial proclamation of 720 says, "The late Taoist priest She Fashan was thoroughly intimate with natural reality, mystically expounded subtle principles, held keys to secrets, and worked wonders. Surely because the unknown is silent and hard to fathom and the imperceptible is immeasurable, while in his feelings he lodged in humble desolation, in his activities he mixed with courtiers. He remained a priest but didn't depend on it; he was given imperial honor yet didn't glory in it. He stood out distinctly as an individual, coolly going his way alone. He overcame temper and detached from desire; his chaste manner was free of pollution. His golden bones stood out externally, his pearl light shone within. Thus he was the embodiment of qualification for immortality, and his repute rose to the highest level of merit. When we were not occupied with administration, we used to ask him about the ultimate Way, while he would offer advice on principles of governing the country. With his participation in planning and private criticism, affairs went well, spreading benefits. We are moved by the fact that his good name has not yet disappeared, while saddened by the brief stay of his physical remains. Let there be no lament at this passing, as he will abide eternally. It is just that we have been feeling sadness in our heart and deem it appropriate to enunciate a courtesy command, to advertise to the underworld. He is to be granted the title of commander in chief of the province of Yue."

SUN SIMIAO

Sun Simiao was a man of Huayuan in the imperial capital. He started studying when he was seven years old, and was able to memorize more than a thousand words a day. By the time he reached his majority he was skilled in discussing *Chuang-tzu, Lao-tzu,* and the doctrines of the hundred philosophers. The supervisor of Luo province, Du Guxin, met him and said in admiration, "This is a sage boy. I only regret that his capacity is great but will be unusable if given small scope."

At that time Emperor Xuan of the Zhou dynasty [r. 578–580] was living in retirement on Great White Mountain[27] because there were

---

27. In Shaanxi, west of the imperial capital of Chang'an, containing the eleventh of the thirty-six minor grotto heavens of Taoism.

so many incidents in the royal family. Emperor-to-be Wen of the Sui dynasty [r. 581–604] was assisting his administration at that time; he summoned Sun to become a college professor, but he claimed to be ill and did not rise to the summons. He once said to a familiar, "After fifty years a sage will emerge; I will help him rescue people."

When Emperor Taizong [of the Tang dynasty] assumed the throne [in 627], he summoned Sun to the capital city. The emperor was impressed by how very young he looked. He said, "I knew he was one who has the Way. He is truly worthy of respect. Certainly Xianmen[28] and Guangcheng[29] weren't talking nonsense!" He was going to confer a title and rank on him, but Sun stoutly refused to accept. In 659 Emperor Gaozong appointed him as a counselor, but he also refused this. In 674 he asked to be allowed to return on account of infirmity. He was given a special gift of a good horse and the residence of the steward for the territory of the Princess of Fanyang to live in. Famous scholars of the time, such as Song Lingwen, Meng Shen, and Lu Zhaolin, formally became his students and waited on him.

Simiao once accompanied an imperial visit to the Jiucheng Palace, and Zhaolin stayed in his house in the meantime. At that time there was a sick pear tree in the yard, and Zhaolin composed an elegy for it; the introduction said, "In 673 I lay ailing in the government residence Abode of Luminous Virtue in Chang'an; the elders say it had been the residence of the steward of the territory of the Princess of Fanyang. The princess died before she was married, so her territory was abolished; but at the time there was a conscientious man, Sun Simiao, to reside there. Master Sun combined the ancient and the modern in his practice and comprehended the arts of calculation in his learning. In terms of lofty discussion of True Unity, he is the old Zhuangzi of Meng;[30] in his profound penetration of nonduality, he is simply a modern Vimalakirti.[31] In his figuring of the calendar and

28. A legendary immortal of ancient times, mentioned in history as having been sought for by the First Emperor of China, who wanted to live forever.
29. A legendary sage who is said to have taught arts of health and longevity to the Yellow Emperor in antiquity.
30. That is, Chuang-tzu, the famous Taoist writer.
31. Vimalakirti is the central character of the *Vimalakirti-nirdesa-sutra*, a widely read Buddhist scripture. Vimalakirti is both a householder and a fully enlightened Buddha, representing the main message of the ultimate nonduality of the absolute and the relative, or the secular and the sacred.

measurement of heaven and earth, he is a peer of Luoxia Hong[32] and Master Anqi."[33]

Zhaolin had a terminal illness that physicians couldn't cure, so he asked Simiao what his way was. Simiao said, "I've heard that those who are good at talking about nature must have asked people about it, while those who are good at talking about humanity base it on nature. Nature has four seasons and five elemental forces, cold and heat alternating; in their cyclic operation, harmony produces rain, rage produces wind, condensation produces frost and snow, expansion produces rainbows. These are constants of sky and earth. Humans have four limbs and five organs, alternately wake and sleep, and breathe in and out, vital energy coming and going; circulating as blood and oxygen, manifesting as mood, emerging as tone of voice, these are normal conditions of humanity. Using the physical by day and using the ethereal by night is common to nature and humanity. When they deviate, heat produces fever, while congestion produces cold; coagulation produces tumors, collapse produces ulcers. Running produces wheezing, exhaustion produces emaciation. Symptoms appear in the face, aberrations act in the body. Extending this to sky and earth is also like this. Thus when the five parallels expand and contract, the stars and planets go off course, the sun and moon are eclipsed, or comets fly, there are symptoms of danger in the sky and earth. When cold and heat are unseasonable, this is the fever and congestion of sky and earth. When rocks stand and the ground heaves, these are tumors of sky and earth; when mountains crumble and earth collapses, these are ulcers of sky and earth. High winds and heavy rains are the wheezing of sky and earth. When rivers run dry, this is the emaciation of sky and earth. Good physicians cure them with medicines and needles, heal them with acupuncture and formulas. Sages harmonize them with supreme virtue, assist them with human service. Therefore the physical body has illnesses that can be cured, sky and earth have disasters that can be stopped."

He also said, "One should be courageous yet careful, well-rounded in intellect while correct in conduct. The *Classic of Poetry* says, 'As if on the edge of an abyss, like walking on thin ice.' This means being

32. Luoxia Hong (ca. 130–70 B.C.E.) was an astronomer who participated in a Han dynasty calendar reform.
33. Anqi Sheng, a semilegendary immortal said to have lived more than a thousand years.

careful. 'Strong, robust warriors, shield and citadel of the nobles and lords.' This means courage. Not being turned around by profit and not being troubled by duty is correctness of conduct. Acting on seeing subtle indications, not waiting all day, is rounded intellect."

Asked again about the essentials of nurturing nature, he replied, "There are fullness and emptiness in nature, there are stagnation and danger in humans; if you aren't careful of yourself you cannot remedy them. Therefore to nurture your nature it is necessary first to know how to be careful of yourself.

"Being careful is based on fear. If gentlemen had no fear they would neglect humaneness and justice; if farmers had no fear they would neglect sowing and reaping; if craftsmen had no fear they would neglect compass and square; if merchants had no fear their money would not grow. If sons had no fear they'd forget filial piety; if fathers had no fear they'd abandon kindness. If ministers had no fear they wouldn't accomplish anything; if rulers had no fear, they wouldn't quell disorder.

"Therefore the highest is fearing the Way, next is fearing nature, next is fearing things, next is fearing people, next is fearing the body. Those who are concerned about their body are not restrained by people. Those who fear for themselves are not controlled by others. Those who are careful about the small are not afraid of the great, those who are cautious about the near are not contemptuous of the far. In this way human tasks are done."

Simiao said of himself, "I was born in 601; now I'm in my ninety-third year." When inquiries about this were made in his native village, everyone said he was hundreds of years old. Considering the fact that he spoke of events of the Zhou [557–581] and Qi [479–501] dynasties as clearly as if seeing them, he must have been more than a hundred years old. Even so, his eyesight and hearing had not declined, and his spirit and presence were very robust. He can be called one of the brilliant and broadly accomplished undying ones of old.

When Wei Cheng and others were commissioned to compose the histories of the five dynasties of Qi [479–501], Liang [502–556], Zhou [557–581], Chen [557–589], and Sui [589–618], they repeatedly called on Simiao when they feared there were omissions. Simiao would relate the information verbally, as if he had been an eyewitness.

When Lu Jiqing, who was to become the steward of the crown prince, was himself still a boy, he asked Simiao about human duties. Simiao said, "Fifty years hence you will rise in rank to regional earl, and my grandson will be a subordinate official; you should take care of yourself." Later Jiqing became inspector of Xuzhou, and Simiao's grandson Pu became chief of Xiao prefecture in Xuzhou. Now, when Simiao first told Jiqing about this, his grandson Pu had not even been born, and yet he knew beforehand that this would happen. Many of his unusual manifestations were of this kind.

He died in 682. He left directions for a simple interment, specifying that no funerary implements be buried with him and no animals be sacrificed at his funeral rites. After more than a month the appearance of his face had not changed; when they picked up the corpse to put it in the casket, it was like empty clothing. People of the time marveled at this.

He wrote commentaries on *Lao-tzu* and *Chuang-tzu*, composed the thirty-scroll *Precious Prescriptions*,[34] and wrote *True Records of Health Maintenance*, *Bedside Letters*, and *Reconciliation of the Three Teachings*,[35] each in one scroll. All of these circulated in his lifetime.

Taoist Arts

ZHOU YINYAO

Zhou Yinyao was styled Xiyuan. He lived on Lake Dongting and Mount Bao.[36] He himself said he was a descendent of Maestro Lu Li.[37] On the mountain was his ancestral Lu Li Village; he said several people of his lineage had attained the Way.

Yinyao thoroughly practiced the art of refinement of the body in absolute yin.[38] He did not alter his activity and rest on account of day or night, did not dress more lightly or heavily on account of heat or cold; he had a lot of strength even without eating and no leakage in spite of drinking.

---

34. *Qianjinfang*, or *Beiji qianjin yaofang*, a most influential medical encyclopedia.
35. The three teachings of Confucianism, Taoism, and Buddhism.
36. Lake Dongting is in upper Hunan; Mount Bao is in Jiangsu.
37. Lu Li was one of the Four Elders who resolved the succession crisis of the early Han dynasty.
38. In the Maoshan sect this term referred to a temporary deathlike state, from which adepts were said to be able to revive, even after years, physically renewed. The implication is that Yinyao's extraordinary capacities are attributed to this practice. See *Declarations of the Realized* in *Daozang jiyao*, vol. 18, p. 7935b.

During the Zhengguan era [627–650], he was summoned to Chang-an, where he was lodged in an inner palace and questioned about the way to train the breathing. He replied, "What I practice is for ordinary people, and its effect does not affect anything. The benefit of one word from an emperor or king is a blessing to everyone; the effects of their attaining the Way quickly affect subjects. My petty studies are nothing a ruler with ten thousand chariots should pay attention to." He earnestly sought to return to the mountain, and the emperor decreed that he have his wish.

Another time, Li Deyu[39] of Zanhuang heard of his way and built the Baoli Sanctuary of Saintly Ancestors Revering the Source as a place to present offerings to him. The sanctuary was in front of the Huayang south cave of Mount Juqu [Maoshan]. There is a record by Linghu Chu.[40]

A Taoist Recluse

TIAN YOUYAN

Tian Youyan was a man of Sanyuan in the capital district. At first he was appointed a college student, then later he dropped out, returned home, and traveled to Great White Mountain. Whenever he came upon woods and springs that pleased him, he'd stay there, unable to leave. His mother and his wife and children all had transcendental aspirations, and they roamed the mountains and rivers with Youyan for more than twenty years.

Later he went into Basket Mountain and built a house to live in on the east side of the shrine to Xu You, calling himself "Xu You's neighbor to the east."[41]

In 679 Emperor Gaozong visited Mount Song. He sent Xue Yuan-chao, attendant gentleman of the Palace Secretariat, to ask after Youyan's mother. Youyan came out in mountain garb and field head-gear to bow; the emperor had his own attendants hold him up and stop him.

39. Li Deyu was a regional inspector and minister under the Tang dynasty.
40. Linghu Chu was a Tang dynasty scholar and regional inspector.
41. That is, Xu You, the legendary recluse of ancient times.

The emperor said to him, "Maestro, you cultivate the Way in the mountains; have you gotten what you want?"

Youyan said, "I am incurably infected by springs and rocks and terminally afflicted by haze and mist. Since I'm living in an enlightened era, I've gotten to roam free."

The emperor said, "How does our finding you now differ from the Han emperor's finding the Four Elders!"[42]

Yuanchao said, "Emperor Gaozong of the Han dynasty wanted to bypass his legitimate son for a bastard; it was only then that Huang and Qi[43] came. How does that compare to Your Majesty's respect for those who are hidden, personally seeking them in mountain caves?" The emperor was extremely pleased by this.

The emperor used the opportunity to take Youyan to the cloister where he was staying on the journey, then cleverly convinced him and his family to go to the capital. He gave him a professorship at the Institute for Honoring Culture and had him talk with the junior mentor of the crown prince, Liu Rengui.[44]

Later, when the emperor was going to build the Sanctuary in Service of Heaven, he traveled to Mount Song. Youyan's old house had already been there next to the cloister site, and the emperor gave special orders not to tear it down. He personally wrote a sign to hang over the doorway saying, "The House of the Recluse Tian Youyan."

Taoist Disposition

LU HONGYI

Lu Hongyi was styled Haoran. He was originally a man of Fanyang but moved his household to Luoyang. He received an education in youth and was quite skilled at calligraphy in four styles: the seal script, the large seal script, the standard script, and the clerical script. He lived in seclusion on Mount Song.[45]

---

42. The Four Elders are introduced in the story of Zhang Liang.

43. These are names of two of the Four Elders.

44. Liu Rengui (602–685) was a chancellor, regent, and general under the Tang dynasty.

45. Mount Song, outside the ancient "eastern capital" Luoyang in Henan, is the central of the five sacred mountains of China. Few Houses Mountain, the legendary birthplace of Chan Buddhism mentioned in earlier stories in this collection, is one of the two main peaks of the Mount Song complex.

In the beginning of the Kaiyuan era [713–741] an emissary was sent with all courtesies, but though summoned twice by the emperor, he didn't go. In 717 an imperial decree was issued saying, "Lacking as we are, disgracefully undertaking an important position, we have lamented the fact that mysticism has long since changed and the influence of purity is not yet in the ascendant; every time we reflect on savants in exile, we wish to hear instructions for emperors. As you have inner virtue and penetrating reason, have found out the profound and arrived at the subtle, thoroughly studied the Way of universal unity, put into practice the virtue of centered equilibrium, you are certainly lofty enough to compare to the ancients. Therefore we have issued letters summoning you, anticipating accord with your excellent accomplishments; yet you have made excuses to decline each time, refusing to come, causing us to wait with empty heart for several years now. Although you succeed in innocent practice of the integrity of a recluse, you're missing the obligation of respect for your late father. Are the purposes of the court on a different course from the people? Are you going to indulge your desire for mountain forests, unable to return? There is an important ethic in courtesy; the manifestations of ruler and subject cannot be abolished. Now, the imperial palace is close by, posing no difficulties, so we have ordered the delivery of a gift of a bundle of silk, with a repeat announcement of this message, hoping to be able to change your behavior to comply with our wish."

Hongyi went in response to the summons, arriving at the eastern capital in 718. When he met the emperor, he didn't bow. The prime minister sent a secretarial receptionist to ask the reason. He reported, "I have heard that Lao-tzu said, 'Ritualism is slightness of sincere faith.' It is not to be relied on. I dared to greet the emperor with sincere faith." The emperor invited him individually up into the inner palace and gave him wine and food.

The emperor decreed, "Lu Hongyi has arrived in response to a summons, and on inquiring of him into the supreme Way, he has been found to be in harmony with the culture of purity, so the liberated man is hereby promoted to encourage the whole land, to be given the position of grand master of remonstrance." Hongyi stoutly refused.

Another imperial proclamation stated, "In ancient times it was in Emperor Yao to keep the integrity of Xu You intact; thinking back to

Great Yu, acknowledging Bocheng's loftiness,[46] we realize that there are those whom emperors cannot make their subjects, whom lords cannot make their companions. 'The meaning of the timing of withdrawal is great indeed!' Lu Hongyi, recluse of Mount Song, has cut off traffic in the remoteness of obscurity, concentrating on reading, living in seclusion to seek his aim, practicing righteousness to attain his way, reclining in the clouds in forested valleys for many years. Does not tradition say, 'Promote detached people, and everyone in the land will be loyal'? So we have sent letters to his mountain cave, summoning and inviting him with every courtesy, in anticipation of his assistance, trying to extend principled government; yet he remains strongly independent, firmly indomitable. He silences himself to control his conduct, cleans his mind to encourage its fluidity. He steadfastly refuses glory and favor so as to enrich his morals; he refuses to lower his aspirations so as to preserve his body. Yan Ziling[47] of Huiji could not be constrained by fame; Wang Pa[48] of Taiyuan ultimately retired on the excuse of illness. Let him freely return to the mountains as grand master of remonstrance, with a yearly allowance of a hundred piculs of rice, and fifty bolts of silk to pay for his medicinal ingredients; have the city and county escort him to his place of seclusion. If he knows when the court is right or wrong, he should let it be known by letter."

When he was about to return to the mountains, the emperor also presented him with clothing for a recluse and a country house. His favor and courtesy were exceptionally attentive. Hongyi composed *Pictures from a Rustic Cottage: Ten Records*, which was transmitted as a treasure by enthusiasts.

46. Bocheng Zigao became a lord in the time of the predynastic king Yao, an idealized sage of Chinese political philosophy. Yao abdicated to Shun, and Shun abdicated to Yu. Yu is the Great Yu cited in the text. When King Yu assumed the throne, Bocheng Zigao renounced his lordship and became a subsistence farmer. Yu sought him out and asked him why he retired. Bocheng replied, "You reward and punish, but the people are still not humane. From here on, virtue will decline; from here on, penal law will rule. The rebellions of future generations will begin from here."
47. Yan Guang.
48. Wang Pa was an aristocrat of the Han dynasty. When Wang Mang usurped the throne in 7 C.E., he renounced his status and cut off all communication with acquaintances in government. When the Han throne was reestablished nearly twenty years later, Wang was asked to become a secretary of state, but he declined and remained in retirement.

A Taoist Scholar

BO LIZHONG

Bo Lizhong was a man of Junyi in Chenliu.[49] He was widely acquainted with literature and history. He used to live in seclusion in the ancient city of Great Liang,[50] so people called him the Philosopher of Liang Hill.

In the Jingyun era [710–712] he was summoned by the emperor and appointed editor, but he eventually quit the office and left. In 729 the chief secretary of the Justice Department, Wang Zhiyin, submitted a memorial commending Lizhong's study in seclusion, maintaining his discipline faithfully in hardship, imbued with the manners of the ancients, suitable for a palace reader in attendance. But when he was summoned to the capital city, Lizhong declined on account of age and infirmity.

The emperor issued a declaration saying, "The scholar in retirement Bo Lizhong, former editor of the Secretariat, is richly learned in the books of Taoism, and his way graces the garden of Confucianism. Searching into the profound, he thereby sees its subtleties; living in seclusion, he is able to attain his aim. So as we were recruiting Confucians, searching for recluses, his plain manner proved lofty by nature, and ceremonial garb is not what he values. Now that he's elderly and approaching the evening of his days, he should be given distinction and rank, made to receive favors mandated as a courtesy, to foster the excellence of favoring savants. He is suitable for grand master for closing court."

Taoist Character

PAN SHIZHENG

Pan Shizheng was styled Zizhen. He was a man of Zongcheng in Beiqin.[51] He lost his mother in youth and camped beside her grave,

---

49. In Henan.
50. A later capital of the ancient state of Wei, located in Henan, governing parts of Shanxi and Henan.
51. In Shandong.

thus becoming known for filial piety. During the Daye era [of the Sui dynasty, 605–616], he was ordained as a Taoist priest. He constantly attended Religious Leader Wang, who transmitted to him all the secrets of Taoism, including talismans and charts.

Shizheng was pure and quiet, with few desires; he lived in Meandering Valley of Mount Song for more than twenty years, consuming only rice infused with medicinal herb juice, pine needles, and water. When Emperor Gaozong [of the Tang dynasty r. 650–683] went to the eastern capital, on coming to that valley he saw him staying alone in silence, with only a simple couch of braided vines, just about rotting away. The emperor asked Shizheng sympathetically, "Here in the mountains, what do you need?" He replied, "What I need are flourishing pines and pure springs. They are not lacking on this mountain." Then the emperor commanded him to draw a talisman. He declined, saying he didn't know how to write talismans. The emperor and empress marveled at him and left.

The next day he was brought by rickshaw to the cloister where the imperial couple was staying on their journey, and they conversed. They kept him at a way station for a while and then let him return. Subsequently the emperor ordered the office in charge to construct a monastery in the place where he lived, to be called Honoring Tang, and to build a separate meditation cloister on the ridge peak for him to stay in. He also had the Sanctuary in Service of Heaven relocated. Another imperial edict ordered the office in charge to construct a special gate at the mouth of Meandering Valley, to be called Gateway to the Wanderings of an Immortal. He also had another gate, Gateway to the Search for the Real, set up on the north front of the garden. All of these were named for Shizheng.

Figuring when the rickshaw would arrive, the master of music presented newly composed musical works. The emperor had him entitle them "Praying to an Immortal," "Hoping for an Immortal," and "Waiting for an Immortal." All told, the emperor presented Shizheng with dozens of poems. He was treated with great honor.

In 682, as he was about to die, he said to his disciples, "I withdrew here in silence but then caused excess toil to the ruler of the world and disturbed the holy mountains. I am truly a criminal. In your study of the Way, you can't be too deep or too subtle."

When he died he was ninety-eight years old. The emperor and empress continued to miss him; they bestowed the title Superior Grand Master of the Palace and the posthumous name Maestro Comprehending Mysticism. They directed Minister of Works Wang Shi to compose his epitaph.

Taoist Arts

LIU DAOHE

Liu Daohe was a man of Wanqiu in Chenzhou.[52] He first went into seclusion on Mount Song with the revered Master Pan. Emperor Gaozong heard of him and ordered the establishment of the Monastery of the Absolute One, where he was secluded, so he could reside there.

He was summoned to the imperial palace numerous times. When he was going to perform a rite in honor of the sky on Mount Tai, it happened to rain for a long time, so the emperor ordered him to work the art of stopping rain in the Sanctuary for Phoenix Gazing. Suddenly the sky cleared; the emperor was delighted and immediately sent a message to go ahead and climb Mount Tai to pray for blessings and divine assistance.

All the gifts the emperor gave him over time, he distributed to the poor. Gaozong once ordered him to compound restorative elixir. When the elixir was done, he presented it to the emperor.

He died in the early 670s. When the emperor had the Sanctuary in Service of Heaven rebuilt, they moved Daohe's crypt; disciples opened the casket to change his clothes and rebury his body, but there was only an empty skin, split on the back, like a cicada that had molted. His teeth and bones were all gone. Everyone said he'd been liberated from the corpse.[53]

When Emperor Gaozong heard this, he lamented, "Reverend Master Liu compounded elixir for us but then took it himself and became immortal!" What he had presented to the emperor turned out to be nothing extraordinary.

52. In Henan.
53. For assorted physical signs of liberation from the corpse as interpreted in Maoshan Taoism, see *Declarations of the Realized* in *Daozang jiyao*, vol. 18, pp. 7395b and 7396a.

Taoist Character

SIMA ZIWEI

Sima Ziwei, also named Chengteng and styled Ziwei, was a man of En, east of the Yellow River. He was a descendant of the Duke of Langye, inspector of Jin province under the Zhou dynasty. He liked studying from youth but was uninterested in becoming an official, so he became a Taoist priest. He attended Pan Shizheng and inherited his talismans and charts and techniques of abstention from grain, energy induction, and taking dietary supplements.

Shizheng found him particularly praiseworthy and extraordinary. He said to him, "I inherited the teachings of True Unity[54] deriving from Recluse Tao; coming to you, you are the fourth generation."

Ziwei traveled around to all the famous mountains, then stayed on Mount Tiantai. Empress Zetian heard of him and called him to the capital, sending down a handwritten decree praising him. Then when he was about to return, she ordered Li Jiao, overseer of the Unicorn Terrace, to give him a send-off party east of the Luo Bridge.

In 711 Emperor Ruizong sent his older brother Cheng Wei to Mount Tiantai to escort Ziwei to the capital city. Once inside the palace, Ziwei was first asked about the technical calculation of yin and yang. He replied, "The *Tao Te Ching* says, 'To practice the Way, reduce day by day; reduce and reduce, until there's nothing to do.' Now then, what the mind and eyes know and see cannot be stopped even if you repeatedly reduce them, so why pursue foreign doctrines in addition, increasing your intellectual thinking?"

The emperor said, "To regulate the body, nondoing is pure and high, but how is nondoing for regulating the nation?"

Ziwei replied, "The nation is like the body. Lao-tzu says, 'Free the mind in serenity, harmonize the mood with the infinite, go along with the inherent nature of things without selfishness toward them, and the land will be orderly.' The *I Ching* says, 'Sages harmonize their virtues with heaven and earth.' So, as we know that heaven is truthful

---

54. The Taoist denomination of True Unity is said to derive originally from Celestial Master Zhang Daoling; eventually it would absorb the streams of Taoism following the scriptures of Higher Purity, Spiritual Jewels, and Three August Ones. Recluse Tao means Tao Hongjing, who strived to construct a comprehensive synthesis of Taoism with Confucianism and Buddhism.

without speaking and fulfills without doing, the doctrine of nondoing is the way to regulate the nation."

The emperor sighed and said, "The advice of Guangcheng[55] was precisely this!"

Ziwei insisted on leaving to return to the mountains, so the emperor sent him off with gifts of a precious lute and a vest with a sun-glow pattern. Distinguished gentlemen of the court presented him with poems. Li Shi sang first, and more than three hundred people joined in. This collection of poetry was entitled *White Cloud Record*.

Lu Zangyong pointed to Mount Zhongnan and said to the maestro, "It's beautiful there; why insist on Tiantai?" He replied, "As I see it, it's a shortcut to serving in office." Zangyong looked embarrassed. It seems he had previously secluded himself on Mount Zhongnan.

In 721 Emperor Xuanzong sent an envoy to invite Ziwei to the capital and personally received a teaching talisman. In 722 the emperor went back to the western capital, and Ziwei asked to return to Tiantai. Xuanzong presented him with poetry as a gift for his journey. In 727 the emperor summoned him back to the capital and ordered him to personally choose a beautiful site on Royal House Mountain[56] to locate a sanctuary where he might reside. Ziwei then informed the emperor that the cave governments of the Five Mountains each had realized people of Higher Purity descending to do their jobs, involving the regulation of the mountains, rivers, wind, and rain, the atmospheric order of yin and yang. Their official uniforms, and the spiritual immortals assisting them, all had designated classifications. He asked the emperor to set up a shrine for rituals as well, to distinguish the spirits of the mountains and forests.

Emperor Xuanzong did as he said and ordered that one shrine to the Lords of Reality be located on each of the Five Mountains. The iconography and design were invented according to ideas suggested by the Taoist scriptures.

Ziwei was skilled at seal and square scripts, and Xuanzong ordered him to copy the classic of Lao-tzu in three forms of calligraphy, on the basis of which an orthodox text would be published. He did a critical edition of 5,380 characters he considered authentic text and presented this to the emperor.

---

55. Legendary teacher of the Yellow Emperor.
56. This is the first of the Ten Great Grotto Heavens.

By imperial decree, his dwelling was named Terrace of Positive Energy. The emperor wrote the nameplate for it himself. He donated three hundred rolls of silk for Ziwei to use to pay for herbs and dietary supplements.

When he was eighty-nine years old, he died on Royal House Mountain. The day his disciples reported his departure, there was a pair of cranes circling the altar, and a white cloud issued from inside the altar, reaching all the way up to the sky. Meanwhile, the master's face looked as if he were alive.

Emperor Xuanzong deeply admired him and issued a statement saying, "Sima Ziwei's mind rested on the supremacy of the Way; his understanding of mysticism was far-reaching. He traveled to all the famous mountains and secretly resorted to the caves of immortals. Contemplating the subtle, he roamed freely in the sphere of self-mastery; returning to the root, he rested peacefully in the realm of nothing whatsoever. Since his name has been registered in the class of immortals and his rank is among the spiritual offices, to be sure, though forests and valleys have not changed, the distant sky is now vast; his words and thoughts were lofty and powerful, and there is sorrow in my heart. He should be given a token of distinction, to light up the annals of alchemy. He is to be given the title of Imperial Aide and Advisor, with the posthumous name Zhenyi, 'Real One.'" The emperor personally composed his epitaph, while Wei Qumou[57] wrote a biography.

Taoist Culture

WU YUN

Wu Yun was styled Zhenjie. He was a man of Huayin prefecture in Huazhou.[58] He mastered the classics in youth and was a good writer. He was recommended for examination in the category of *advanced scholar*, but he didn't pass. High-minded and pure by nature, he didn't have anything to do with common vulgarities. He went into Mount Song, became a Taoist priest following the Reverend Master Pan, and inherited the teachings of True Unity. He studied intensely and mastered all the techniques.

---

57. Wei Qumou (749–801) was a noted poet.
58. In Shaanxi.

During the Kaiyuan era [713–741] he traveled south to Jinling and inquired into the Way at Maoshan. After a long time at this, he traveled to Tiantai, where he gazed on the ocean and associated with famous gentlemen. His literary work reached the capital, and Emperor Xuanzong, hearing of his repute, sent for him. Once he arrived, he was ordered into the Hall of Great Concord. The emperor conversed with him and was very pleased; he appointed him attendant scholar.

One day the emperor asked him about Taoist arts. He replied, "For the essence of Taoist arts, nothing compares to the *Tao Te Ching*. As for the ornate language and extensive verbiage of other works, they just waste paper."

The emperor also asked about the cultivation of spiritual immortality. He replied, "This is something for rustics and requires years of effort seeking it; it is not something rulers should ask about."

Yun's expositions were always conventional doctrines of worldly matters. He used subtle expressions to voice criticism, and the emperor appreciated this. He bestowed the honorific name Head of Religion on him.

During the Tianbao era [742–755], when Li Linfu[59] and Yang Guozhong[60] were in charge of affairs, political and social order became increasingly tangled day by day. Yun insistently sought to return to Mount Song but was not permitted to do so in spite of repeated petitions. Then the emperor ordered that a separate cloister be built at a mountain monastery.

When An Lushan was about to start a civil war, Yun sought to return to Maoshan and was allowed to do so. Once the central plain had been plunged into chaos, there were lots of bandits in the Yangzi and Huai

59. Li Linfu (d. 752) was chancellor under Emperor Xuanzong (r. 712–755). He is execrated for attempting to isolate the emperor from officials and for promoting the appointment of non-Chinese to positions of military command. He was close to An Lushan, one such commander, who staged a disastrous rebellion against the Tang dynasty in 755.

60. Yang Guozhong (d. 756) was a political rival of Li Linfu. He also became chancellor, and held many other titles as well, through his family relation with the emperor's favorite consort. His incompetence as chancellor is considered a major impetus for the rebellion of An Lushan, and his incompetence in military strategy is blamed for the fall of the capital city to An Lushan's forces.

river regions, so he traveled east to Tiantai and Shanzhong,[61] where he formed nonpartisan friendships with Li Bo[62] and Kong Chaofu.[63]

His collected writings comprise twenty scrolls; Quan Deyu[64] wrote a preface for them. His *Three Works on Mysticism, Treatise on the Possibility of Learning Spiritual Immortality,* and other works were praised by knowledgeable scholars.

When Yun was in the imperial academy, he was treated with particular favor. Gao Lizhi[65] liked Buddhism, so he once slighted Yun in the presence of the emperor and insistently sought his ejection. But the logic of Yun's statements was far-reaching and profound, while the literary quality of his writing was brilliant; whenever he composed a work, people would vie to make copies of it. With the freedom of Li Bo and the heroic elegance of Du Fu,[66] it seems only Yun could combine the two.

Taoism and Authority

Li Bi

Li Bi was styled Changyuan. He originally lived in Demon Valley. At the age of seven he knew how to write compositions, and in 728 he was summoned to meet the emperor as an *extraordinary child.* He was most favored by Zhang Jiuling,[67] who called him his little friend.

When he grew up, he studied widely and became expert in the *I Ching.* He used to travel around to Mount Song, Mount Hua, and Mount Zhongnan, seeking the spiritual immortals' art of not dying.

During the Tianbao era [742–755], he went to the imperial establishment and presented *Proposal for Restoring the Yellow Emperor's*

---

61. In Zhejiang.
62. Li Bo is one of the most famous poets in Chinese history.
63. Kong Chaofu was a leading Confucian scholar, a thirty-seventh generation descendant of Confucius.
64. Quan Deyu (759–818) was a distinguished statesman and scholar.
65. A powerful eunuch at Xuanzong's court.
66. Du Fu is commonly cited along with Li Bo as one of the greatest poets in Chinese history. Du Fu is known for sobriety, Li Bo for intoxication.
67. Zhang Jiuling (678–740) was a scholar and poet who held a number of high positions under the Tang dynasty, including director of the Secretariat and grand councillor.

Nine Cauldrons. The emperor, considering him quick-witted, had him lecture on Lao-tzu. He had a command of the principles and obtained the position of attendant scholar.

When Xiaozong assumed the throne at Lingwu in 756, he was making inquiries searching for him when Bi showed up on his own. Once he had interviewed him, the emperor was pleased, having had the successes and failures of the empire set forth to him. He was going to give Bi an official post, but Bi stoutly refused. Instead he asked to be allowed to attend discussions of national affairs as a guest and join the imperial entourage on excursions. Everyone pointed and said, "The priest is the ruler, while the layman is the hermit."

Thus the emperor bestowed the gold seal and purple cord of court rank upon him and appointed him minister of war for the Infantry of the Chief Commander, king of Guangping.

The emperor once said, "You wait on the deities above, you are our teacher in the center, and now you judge the infantry of Guangping below. Thus are we, father and son [emperor and king] sustained by the principles of your Way." Cui Yuan[68] and Li Fuguo[69] were jealous of the closeness and confidence Bi enjoyed. Bi feared there would be trouble and requested retirement on Mount Heng. An imperial decree provided him with a salary of a third-ranked official, presented him with the outfit of a retired gentleman, and prepared a dwelling for him on Mount Lu.

Bi once took a curved pine branch to use as a backrest, calling it "fostering balance." Later he found one shaped like a dragon, which he presented to the emperor. All around vied to imitate this.

When Daizong became emperor [in 763], he summoned Bi and housed him in the library of Penglai Hall. At first he didn't eat meat, but since rank was bestowed on him he was forced to eat meat by imperial decree.

When Dezong [r. 780–805] was at the Sanctuary in Service of Heaven, he summoned Bi to his temporary headquarters and appointed him policy adviser. Bi first had a road cut through the mountains to the Triple Gate [sluices of the Yellow River] to facilitate shipping. Because

68. Cui Yuan was a regional inspector and officer of the Secretariat under Emperor Suzong (r. 756–762).
69. Li Fuguo (704–762) was a eunuch who held high offices in the department of the military under Emperor Suzong.

of this effort, he was promoted to minister of rites, then in three years to associate manager of affairs.

The emperor once casually remarked, "Lu Qi[70] was puritanical and outspoken, but he had little learning and could not broaden us with the ancient Way. Everyone pointed out his treachery, but we never noticed."

Bi replied, "Had Your Majesty been able to sense Qi's evil, how could the troubles of the Jianzhong era[71] have occurred? Li Kui[72] combined the foreign commanders of Chinese armies, while Yan Zhenqing[73] used Xilie. The damage done to longstanding benevolence and goodwill was great indeed.

"Also, Yang Yan[74] was condemned, though not executed; Lu Qi brought about his downfall and made Guan Bo[75] minister. When Li Huaiguang[76] became successful, Lu Qi goaded him into revolt. This is deceiving heaven."

The emperor said, "What you say happened, true enough, but you must know what Sang Damo[77] said about the chaos of the Jianzhong era, that it was destined to be so?"

Bi replied, "So-called destiny is something said after the fact. Leaders make destiny; they shouldn't plead destiny. If you plead destiny, then there's no rewarding good and no punishing evil!"

The emperor said, "I'll try not to say 'destiny' anymore."

Shortly he was made a scholar of the Library Honoring Literature, working on national history. Bi requested that the first day of the cy-

70. Lu Qi was prime minister under Emperor Dezong, who is faulted for judging people on appearances.

71. This refers to a rebellion of regional authorities. The Jianzhong era lasted from 780 to 784.

72. Li Kui (711–784) held numerous offices under the Tang dynasty, including commissioner for entry into alliance with Tufan. Tufan was a Tibetan state considered a major threat to Tang dynasty China.

73. Yan Zhenqing (709–785) commanded several successful battles against the rebel An Lushan and served in a number of posts under the Tang dynasty, including minister of works and minister of justice. When Li Xilie rebelled, Lu Qi sent Yan to negotiate a surrender, intending to encompass Yan's death. Yan stood up to Li's threats and won the latter's respect. Yan was later assassinated.

74. Yang Yan (727–781) was briefly a minister of state for Emperor Dezong. He is noted for reforming the tax system.

75. Guan Bo held many posts under the Tang dynasty. He is said to have been promoted for prime minister by Lu Qi because the latter considered him easy to control.

76. A regional inspector.

77. A famous prognosticator.

cle of the second lunar month be made the Day of Harmony in the Center[78] instead of the last day of the lunar cycle of the first month and that on that occasion the great ministers be given *royal relative residence rulers*, signifying the sizing up of bureaucrats. He presented a book on agriculture to teach basic production. The emperor was very pleased and issued an order making the second day of the second month, the third day of the third month, and the ninth day of the ninth month three official holidays, when everyone was to be given a bonus of a string of a thousand cash and invited to a banquet.

In the eighth month of 788, the sun eclipsed the two stars associated with literature and culture. Bi said, "Those stars govern maps and books; among the great ministers there will be someone aggrieved. Since I'm both a managing minister and a scholar, it must be me." The next year, as it turned out, he died.

Bi had free access to the imperial palace, and he worked for four emperors, so he was the object of the jealousy of crafty sycophants numerous times, yet he always escaped by his wits. Moreover, time and again there were factional plots, of which he was able to alert the emperor, and he also improved and enlightened government himself. The restoration of the two capitals praised by historian Liu Bi was due in large part to the planning of Li Bi; his contribution was even greater than Lu Lian's[79] and Fan Li's.

Taoist Character

LI HANGUANG

Li Hanguang was a man of Jiangdou in Guangling.[80] His original surname was Hong, but he changed it in deference to Empress Zetian. He came from a family of hereditary professional scholars. His father Xianwei, titled Professor of Chaste Seclusion, was expert in the Huang-Lao arts.

In 705 Hanguang was ordained as a Taoist priest by virtue of his pure conduct and lived at Dragon Rising Monastery. In 729 he apprenticed himself to Sima Ziwei on Royal House Mountain. One day Sima looked at him and said, "You have the appearance of the jadelike

---

78. On this occasion the emperor customarily gave a banquet for the ministers of state.
79. That is, Lu Zhonglian.
80. In Jiangsu.

purity of the realized ones." Li Hanguang lived on the south side of
Mount Song for more than twenty years.

When Sima became immortal and left, Emperor Xuanzong summoned Hanguang to the palace and conversed with him. The emperor
said admiringly, "Now that I've seen Hanguang, I know the realized
man Sima is still in the world."

One day the emperor asked about the cauldron of gold. Hanguang
replied, "The virtues of the Way are public; ascension is a private
matter within the public, that's all. Sometimes we see the private, but
a ruler maintains education—if he seeks eternal life and inquires after
his desires, then that is like trying to tie down the wind." Xuanzong
was deeply impressed and marveled at him. He had him stay at the
monastery Terrace of Positive Energy for more than a year; then
Hanguang pleaded illness and asked to return to Maoshan to compile
and edit the scriptural teachings.

In 745 the emperor ordered a commissioner to deliver a letter bearing the imperial seal summoning Hanguang. When he came, he was
lodged in the palace. Whenever the emperor wanted to ask him questions, the emperor would always fast and bathe first. When the emperor requested transmission of Taoist methods, he declined on the
grounds of illness and again sought to return to the mountains.

So the emperor issued a decree that he should be accommodated at
the Monastery of Purple Positive Energy, in the former abode of Yang
and the Xus [on Maoshan]. The emperor gave him a collection of poems as a parting gift and prohibited fishing and hunting on the mountain, denying entry to meat eaters.

At that time the scriptures, statements, and records of the realized
ones were already largely scattered and lost. Obeying an imperial order
to search them out, Hanguang found a full complement of precious
writings and presented them to the throne. The emperor also called
the mountain man Wang Min to request Hanguang to write out thirteen pages of the scriptures of Higher Purity in clerical calligraphy to
fill in lacunae. Agreeing, he said, "If you wish to obtain the handwriting of spiritual immortals, just continue generation after generation."

In 748 Emperor Xuanzong received the scriptures and talismans of
the three canons[81] in the Hall of Great Concord, paying respects from

---

81. That is, three Taoist canons: the Higher Purity (Shangqing), Spiritual Jewel (Lingbao) and Three August Ones (San Huang) scriptures. These traditions were all absorbed into the True Unity denomination of Taoism.

afar to his preceptor, giving him the title Master of Mystic Silence and presenting him with a ceremonial robe in order to show the courtesy of a disciple to a teacher.

On the fourteenth day of the eleventh month of 769, Hanguang passed away sitting at the cloister of Purple Positive Energy, holding a book as if he were alive. He was eighty-seven years old at the time. As Grand Master of Mysticism of the Left he was given the title Grand Master of Moral Rectification.

Yan Zhenqing and Liu Shi[82] composed his epitaph and also had twenty-four imperial decrees of the Kaiyuan era[83] in the emperor's handwriting engraved in stone.

Taoist Culture

Zhang Zhihe

Zhang Zhihe was originally named Kuiling; he was a man of Jinhua in Dongyang.[84] His father Youchao was fond of the Way; he mastered the books of Chuang-tzu and Lieh-tzu and wrote a number of essays, such as "The Formless" and "White Horse Proof" to assist their explication.

Zhihe's mother Liu dreamed that a maple tree grew from her belly; then she gave birth to Zhihe. When he was sixteen he was selected for his understanding of the classics; using the examination questions to appeal to Emperor Xiaozong, he obtained a position as scholar in attendance and was given the office of administrative supervisor of the Imperial Insignia Guard.

Later, after his parents died, he no longer served in government. Living by rivers and lakes, he called himself the Fisherman of the Misty Waves. He wrote *Philosopher of Mystic Reality* in twelve scrolls, from which he derived his epithet. He also wrote *Great Changes* in twelve chapters, which contained 365 symbols.

His elder brother Haoling, defender of Puyang, feared he'd flee society, never to return, so he built him a house in the eastern suburbs of Huiji. It was thatched with raw straw; the ridge and roof beams weren't

---

82. Liu Shi served as a reviewer of state documents, a supernumerary official of the state farm system, and a scholar of the imperial academy.
83. From 713 to 741, approximately the first two-thirds of the reign of Emperor Xuanzong.
84. In Shandong.

shaved. With a leopard-skin mat and wooden clogs, he shut the door for ten years.

When Censor in Chief Chen Shaoyou, inspector of Eastern Zhejiang, went to visit him, he was allowed to stay all day. He labeled his dwelling Mystic Reality, and the neighborhood Picture Window Lane. He also had a bridge to his dwelling built; those who went called it the Grand Master's Bridge. Subsequently he wrote a statement "Announcing the Grand Master's Bridge" in appreciation.

Drumming the boat boards with an oar, he went where he pleased. He fished without bait, his object not being to catch fish. Emperor Xiaozong once gave him a manservant and a maidservant; Zhihe had them marry, naming the husband Fish Helper and the wife Firewood Kingfisher. When people asked why, he said, "Fish Helper I have hold the rod and reel the line and row in the reeds; Firewood Kingfisher I have cut orchids, make kindling of cinnamon, and brew tea in bamboo."

Lu Yu,[85] or Jinglingzi, and Pei Xiu,[86] editor, asked, "Who comes to visit you?" He replied, "Space is the house where we live together, the bright moon is a lamp that shines on us all; I have never been apart from the gentlemen everywhere—how could there be coming and going!"

When Yan Zhenqing was inspector of Wuxing, Zhihe came to call on him. Seeing how dilapidated his boat was, Yan asked if he could replace it for him. Zhihe said, "If you give me a fishing boat, I'll make it a floating home, going up and down the rivers and lakes, coming and going in the reeds and rain. This would be good fortune for the rustic!" His humor and quickness of wit were always like this.

He liked to paint landscapes. When he was in his cups he might beat a drum, play a flute, make his brush dance and send ink flying, composing with the rhythm.

Emperor Xiaozong wanted to illustrate Zhihe's *Fishing Songs* but was unable to evoke them effectively. For the censor Li E Zhihe executed a pictorial screen so highly articulated that all who looked at it stared in amazement. Those present on the occasion, more than sixty people, each wrote his name, title, and hometown on the bot-

85. Lu Yu (733–804) was an expert on tea.
86. Pei Xiu (n.d.) served as an editor in the Secretariat (*jiaoshulang*) and as a district commander.

tom. Zhihe made brief notes on all of them, making matching lines underneath for each. Everyone there was astounded.

Nevertheless, by nature he was solitary and inaccessible, impossible either to approach or to alienate. Therefore Mr. Yan wrote in his epitaph, "He looked upon carriages and finery as like refuse, he shut out indulgence and craving like mud. He sought the trail of stalwarts of the Way, in accord with the ancient masters." Li Deyu[87] also praised him for being secluded though famed, distinguished yet having no agenda, neither frustrated nor fulfilled, comparable to Yan Guang.

HE ZHIZHANG

He Zhizhang was a man of Yongxing in Huiji. He was already famous for his writing in youth, nominated for *advanced scholar*, and with the recommendation of Lu Xiangxian[88] he was promoted from doctor of the National Academy to doctor of court ceremonial, then through successive posts up to vice director of the Ministry of Rites, plus scholar of the Institute for Assembling Savants; and he also served as attendant reader to the crown prince.

In 725, when Emperor Xuanzong was going to perform rites dedicated to heaven on Mount Tai, he ordered Zhizhang to explain the ritual. So he reported, "The sky god, the Lord on High, is in the position of the ruler; the Five Lords of the five directions are in the position of subjects. While the designations of the lords vary, ruler and subjects still differ in rank. Your Majesty sacrifices in the position of the ruler on the altar, while the ministers sacrifice in the position of subjects below the altar. In truth this is enough to send a message to future generations; it is an important, exceptional rite. Now the ritual is consummated with three offerings, and the ranks ultimately join in one place."

The emperor said, "That's just how I want to do it; I only asked you as a formality." Now he commanded that the three offerings be performed on a higher stage, while services for the lords of the

---

87. Minister to Emperor Wuzong (r. 840–846), Li Deyu is noted for helping the emperor to limit the power of eunuchs and for commanding a campaign against the Uighurs.

88. Lu served as manager of affairs in the Imperial Secretariat.

five directions and the assembly of spirits were performed on a lower stage.

Later he was assigned to be imperial advisory attaché to the crown prince and director of the palace library.

Zhizhang was naturally free-spirited, good at conversation and humor, admired by all the savants of the time. In 744, while he was sick he had a dream that he traveled to the abode of the gods; then he petitioned the emperor to be ordained a Taoist priest. Requesting permission to return to his native place, he converted his original house into a monastery. Earlier he had petitioned that an area of Yongzhou Lake be made into a wildlife preserve, and this was granted. By imperial decree the monastery was named Thousand Autumns. His son Zeng, manager of interior maintenance, was appointed minister of war for Huiji prefecture in order to make it convenient for him to provide support.

The emperor composed poetry as a present for the journey, with a preface that said, "In 744 He Zhizhang, attaché to the crown prince, reflecting the wisdom of stopping at sufficiency, has announced his retirement, leaving office and renouncing prosperity, aiming to go into the mountains. Considering that he has long been so inclined and now he is getting old, we therefore approve his resignation and allow him to go free. On the fifth day of the first month he is going to return to the mountains of Huiji, so we present him with a parting gift for the road east and hereby order the six ministers, department chiefs, and three administrative grand masters to set up a tent camp at the southeast gate of Chang-an, in consideration of the distance of his journey. This is not only in honor of his virtue and out of respect for his age but also to inspire ordinary society and encourage people and not let the two Su [brothers, exemplars of timely retirement] be the only lights of Chinese history. Now we present poetry as a parting gift; those present at this party should all chime in:

> "Abandoning prosperity to go into the mountains,
> Leaving in old age, finally he pulls out his hatpin.
> Not that we don't value savants,
> But what about their lofty minds?
> Within the realm he got the secret keys;

Beyond convention he releases his hidden heart.
There is only parting at the gate
Where the nobles gaze sadly into the distance."

Everyone from the crown prince on down gave him parting gifts.

Now he called himself the Crazy Stranger of Siming. He was also called Outside Supervisor of the Secretariat. His behavior became most eccentric in the evening of his life, when he would wander about village and town, always getting drunk and leaving poetry behind, without punctuation. He was particularly good at cursive and clerical scripts, as famous as Zhang Xu of Wujun.[89]

He returned to his native place to take care of his health in old age and died in his eighty-sixth year.

Emperor Xiaozong, because of their relationship in the past when he was attendant reader, issued a proclamation in 758 stating, "The late Taoist priest He Zhizhang of the Monastery of a Thousand Autumns was calm and serene, with a gentle and refined heart; his spirit was pure, his will independent, his learning rich, and his capacities strong. Outstanding among the fine bamboo of Huiji, embosoming the fine jade of the Kunlun, he thus caused his name to fly to the province of immortals while lecturer in attendance at the Dragon Tower. Usually quiet and silent to cultivate relaxation, he used conversation and humor to satirize and criticize. Retiring from office on account of advanced age, he showed his sincerity a second time, wishing to follow in the footsteps of the two elders,[90] finally becoming a traveler in Siming. Permitted to fulfill his original aspiration, he shed his court costume and rode off on a dark ox, never to return, going away forever like the white seagull. He never came out of seclusion, but relics renew memories of him; the feeling of old friendship is imbued with a deep sense of mourning. A lavish ceremony should be

89. Zhang Xu lived during the Tang dynasty. Famous for his cursive calligraphy, he was also known for heavy drinking and eccentric behavior. It is said that he used to write with a lock of his own hair dipped in ink. In his time he was called Crazy Zhang and also the Wizard of the Cursive Script. During the reign of Emperor Wenzong of Tang, 827–840, the cursive calligraphy of Zhang Xu was classed with the poetry of Li Bo (subject of the next story) and the sword dance of Pei Min, the three artists being collectively referred to as the Three Incomparables.
90. This may refer either to Bo Yi and Shu Qi or to Laozi (Lao-tzu) and Lao Lai.

given in his honor, to show sorrow and respect. He is to be granted the title of Minister of Rites."

Li Bo

Li Bo was styled Taibo. He was a man of Shandong. He had extraordinary talent in youth; he was broad-minded and free-spirited, detached, with a mind beyond the world.

His father was commandant of Rencheng, so he made his home there.

Bo was perceptive. When he was traveling in Bingzhou, he recognized Guo Ziyi, king of Fenyang, in the army and called him a man among men.

Yet his inclination was to admire the arts of the Way, and he considered it possible to attain spiritual immortality. He wouldn't read books that were not by sages and was ashamed to compose licentious works, so his words often resembled the expressions of celestial immortals. He has been called the greatest poet in history since the classical era.

When he was young he lived in seclusion on Mount Zulai with Confucians from the state of Lu—Kong Chaofu, Han Jun, Pei Zheng, Zhang Shuming, and Tao Mian. Singing in their cups, they drank freely. Contemporaries called them the Six Eccentrics.

During the Tianbao era [742–755] he traveled to Huiji and went into seclusion in Yan with the Taoist priest Wu Yun. Then when Emperor Xuanzong summoned Yun to the capital city, Yun recommended Li Bo to the emperor, who sent an envoy to summon Bo to come in and meet and converse. The emperor had him fed on a couch of seven treasures and made him an imperial scholar in attendance along with Yun.

Bo was already addicted to wine, so when Xuanzong wanted to compose a new song and called for him, Bo was already lying drunk in a tavern. Called in, he washed his face, then was ordered to take up his brush. In a short while he produced three stanzas of lyrics on the subject of an era of peace. The emperor appreciated this.

Once when he was drunk in the audience hall, he tripped Gao Lishi[91] and caused his shoe to come off. Because of this he was de-

---

91. Gao Lishi was a powerful court eunuch.

nounced and ejected. After that he roamed the rivers and lakes, sunk in drink all day long.

At that time Attendant Censor Cui Zongzhi, banished to Jinling, sang and drank with Li Bo. Once they rode a boat from Caishi to Jinling; Bo was wearing a brocade court robe in the boat, gazing about and whistling in amusement, oblivious of everyone else around him.

The first time He Zhizhang met Li Bo, he said in appreciation of him, "This is a banished immortal from heaven above."

Sima Ziwei also said Bo had the manner of immortals and the bones of the Way and could travel with spirits beyond the bounds of the universe.

Later, on a request made through his great-uncle Yan Yun, chief inspector of Chenliu, to Celestial Teacher Gao of Beihai, Li Bo was given a Taoist chart at the Sanctuary of the Purple Absolute in Qizhou. Making a blue patterned hat and waistcoat, he headed east to return to Penglai, after all an immortal ascending to the Cinnabar Hall.[92] He was popularly made out to be the spirit of the evening star. One of his epithets was Realized Man of Higher Purity Mirroring Liberty.

Taoist Arts

MENG SHEN

Meng Shen was a man of Liang in Ruzhou.[93] Recommended for *advanced scholar*, in the late 680s he was successively promoted, up to chamberlain of the Secretariat.

Shen was fond of esoteric arts. When [to-be emperor] Xiaozong was in the provinces, he summoned Shen to be attendant reader; in the capital city of Chang'an he was made inspector of Tangzhou and given the title Honorary Grand Master of the Court, an imperial aide and advisor.

In 705 he returned to the mountains of Yiyang[94] to attend to medicine and diet.

Even in his later years, Shen grew ever stronger in willpower. He once said to familiars, "Those who can preserve the body and nurture

92. That is to say, an exiled immortal finally returning to the realm of immortals.
93. In Henan.
94. In Henan.

nature should always speak good words and have good medicine in hand."

When Ruizong assumed the throne [in 710], he summoned Shen to the capital and was going to give him an important function, but Shen firmly refused on account of infirmity in old age. The emperor issued a special decree that he be presented with all sorts of items and ordered that he be supplied with mutton, wine, and gruel every spring and autumn.

During the Kaiyuan era [713–741], the governor of Henan, Pi Jiang, considering Shen to have the manner of the ancients, renamed his dwelling place Fortune-Teller Village.

Shen died in his ninety-third year. He wrote *Family Rituals and Manners* in one scroll on each topic, and *Prescriptions for Supplementing Nourishment* in three scrolls.

ZHANG GUO

Zhang Guo: it is not known where he was from. He wrote *Mystic Interpretation of the Classic on Hidden Correspondences*,[95] exhaustively elucidating its mystical principles. Later he was given an imperial grand master title of an aide and advisor and dubbed Professor Penetrating Mysteries.

Taoist Silence

ZHU TAOCUI

Zhu Taocui was a man of Chengdu in Yizhou.[96] Detached, taciturn, and unworldly, he dressed in leather, and no one could fathom his actions.

Administrator Dou Gui[97] saw him and sent him a suit of clothes, deerskin headgear, and roebuck shoes, pressing him to take up the role

95. *Yinfujing.* This highly regarded work is interpreted in very different ways. For an interpretation in terms of personal development, see *Commentary on the Classic on Yin Convergence* translated in *Vitality, Energy, Spirit: A Taoist Sourcebook* by Thomas Cleary (1991).

96. In Sichuan.

97. Dou Gui was a prefectural administrator during the Sui dynasty. He joined up with the founder of the Tang dynasty and stopped brigandage in Sichuan. Under the Tang dynasty he was appointed major general of the imperial guard and supreme commander of a redesignated administrative district in Sichuan.

of community leader. He left the clothes on the ground and wouldn't wear them. He built another hermitage in the mountains and covered himself with tree leaves, never accepting any gifts sent to him.

He used to weave straw sandals and set them by the road; those who saw them would say, "These are Layman Zhu's sandals." He bartered them for tea; people would put some there in place of the sandals, taking them away, so he never interacted with anyone. The sandals he made were of soft and fine straw, with dense coils and tight knotting, so people were eager to wear them.

When Gao Shilian[98] was administrator, he invited Zhu courteously and came down the steps to talk to him. Zhu didn't reply but just looked him in the eye and left. Shilian bowed again and said, "Would the elder have me govern Shu[99] by having no concerns?" So Gao simplified the laws and lightened taxes, and the province became very peaceful.

The administrator repeatedly sent people to ask after Zhu, but as soon as he'd see them he'd run into the woods and hide.

Taoist Arts

WANG XIYI

Wang Xiyi was a man of Deng prefecture in Xu province.[100] Alone and poor, he liked the Way. When his parents died, he herded sheep for someone to earn enough for funeral expenses. When their funerals were done, he went into seclusion on Mount Song. For nearly forty years his teacher was the Taoist priest Huang Yi, who transmitted all of his arts of breath control, energy induction, and cultivation.

When Yi died, Wang moved to Mount Zulai in Yanzhou,[101] where he formed a retirees' friendship with the Taoist priest Liu Xuanbo. He liked the *I Ching* and the *Lao-tzu*, and ate pine and cedar needles and mixtures of powdered flowers. As of the Jinglong era [707–710], when he was more than seventy years old, he was more robust than ever.

The regional inspector Lu Qiqing went to call on him and pay respects, taking the opportunity to inquire about the art of governing

98. Gao Shilian (576–647) was chancellor and advisor to Emperor Taizong.
99. Ancient name for Chengdu, center of Sichuan.
100. In Shandong.
101. In Shandong.

people. Xiyi said, "Confucius declared that what you don't want yourself you should not inflict on others—this can be practiced all of your life."

When Emperor Xuanzong toured the East, he commanded the provincial authorities to summon Xiyi courteously before the imperial carriage. He was already ninety-six years old. The emperor ordered the Secretariat director Zhang Shuo to ask about the principles of the Way. Eunuchs escorted him into the imperial chambers, and conversation with him was very pleasing to the emperor.

In 726 the emperor issued a statement saying, "An independent gentleman of Xu province, Wang Xiyi, divorced pedantry and abandoned intellectualism; embracing unity, maintaining integrity, he long ago departed the clamor and dust, going alone to forests and valleys. We extended him courtesies in the palace, impatient to publicize his sagacity, excited at the thought of his coming, and forced him to respond to the invitation. Though far from the tracks of Qili Ji,[102] he has already passed the age of Fu Sheng;[103] it is appropriate to decree that he be ranked among the revered scholars, given the same status as those advanced in years. He is approved for grand master for closing court and doctor of the National University but is allowed to retire and return to the mountains, where the provincial authorities are to deliver a bundle of silk along with wine and meat in spring and autumn, and he is now to be presented with a suit of clothes and twelve hundred yards of silk."

Taoist Silence

WU YOUXU

Wu Youxu was a son of Wu Weiliang, an older brother of Empress Zetian [r. 684–705]. He was placid and had few desires and was fond of the *I Ching* and the book of *Chuang-tzu*. When he was young he

---

102. One of the Four Elders. The Four Elders are mentioned several times in this work as icons of recluses assisting the integrity of government.

103. When the Chinese classics destroyed by the First Emperor were reconstructed from memory in the early Han dynasty, Fu Sheng, who was more than ninety years old at the time, was the scholar consulted for the classic *Ancient Documents*.

changed his name and told fortunes in the markets of Chang-an; when he got cash, he'd leave it there and go away.

When the empress took over command, she enfeoffed him as king of Anping county, but he firmly declined, asking to live in seclusion. The empress suspected that he was faking, so she gave him permission in order to observe what he would do.

Youxu took up residence in a mountain cabin, like a simple hermit. The empress sent his older brother Youxuan to remonstrate with him, but he wouldn't be moved. So the empress finally realized he was unusual.

He stayed around Dragon Gate and Few Houses; in winter he sheltered in thatch and prickly ash, in summer he lived in caves. Imperial gifts of gold and silver vessels and expensive country attire, and the things sent by the kings and nobles—deerskin clothes, silk bandannas, cups carved of tree knobs, and so on, all gathered dust, as he didn't use them.

In his later years he became emaciated, his eyes had a purple light, and he could see stars in the daytime. He died without illness in 723.

When the Wus were at the height of their power, Youxu didn't act opportunistically and never went through their tribulations.[104]

A Taoist Recluse

QIN XI

Qin Xi was a man of Huiji in Yue province. During the rebellion of An Lushan [in 755] he went to Yanzhong[105] to avoid the chaos. Later he put up in Nan'an, Quan province.[106]

There was a certain Nine Sun Mountain, with more than a hundred giant pines that were said to have been planted in the time of the Eastern Jin dynasty [317–419]. Xi built a hut underneath them, hollowed out a rock for an inkstone, and wrote a commentary on *Lao-tzu*, not

---

104. Many members of the Wu family were executed by order of the empress Wu Zetian. They were her relatives, but she cracked down on those who used their family connection for personal ambitions and corrupt purposes, a phenomenon that had fostered problems in court politics for many centuries.
105. In Jiangsu.
106. In Fujian.

coming out for a whole year. The regional inspector Xue Bo went to see him several times and sent mutton and wine every season, but Xi never once went to the city.

After that he moved east to Moling and went into seclusion on Maoshan. He was more than eighty years old. The people of Nan'an were concerned about him and built him a place to stay, calling the mountain Peak of the Eminent Gentleman.

Taoist Character

ZHANG YUN

Zhang Yun was styled Zangzhen. He was a man of Jinyang.[107] Where he lived was in the mountains of Hongzhou,[108] so he was called the Maestro of the Cliffs of Hong. He was six feet nine inches tall,[109] and his beard and eyebrows were outstanding. He was skilled at the lute and calligraphy and was a good whistler.

During the Kaiyuan era [713–741] the emperor [Xuanzong] summoned him for an audience at Brimming Dew Hall and bestowed on him the rank of chamberlain for court ceremonies, adding on other posts up to minister of education. Refusing, he said, "How could Your Majesty begrudge a hill or a valley, preventing your subject from following in the footsteps of Chao and You?"[110]

Returning to the mountains, he ingested energy and abstained from grain. He liked to collect old things. He used to ride a white mule and had five attendants. He used to consume oranges, chestnuts, arrowroot, pomelo, and atractylodes. He had a huge umbrella, a six-cornered fan, a square wood table, a boxwood scepter, antique decorative vases, and such things. As he went in and out of society wearing a red robe and a wisteria hat, to look at him one would think him a real spirit man.

The books he wrote were commentaries on *Lao-tzu*, the *I Ching*, the *Classic of Manners*, and the *Guliang Annals; Records of Hedong*

---

107. In Shanxi.
108. In Jiangxi.
109. Seven *chi* nine *cun*, calculated using Tang dynasty measures.
110. Chao and You refer to Chao Fu and Xu You, who represent high-minded refusal of political power.

in thirty scrolls; and *Praise of the Great Zhou* in ten scrolls. The *Annals of Yuzhang* says, "During the Kaihuang era [581–600] of Sui, Yuzhang was changed to Hongzhou. The maestro seems to have been a man with the Way from ancient times who reappeared during the Sui and Tang dynasties." According to *Announcements of the Realized,* "The Maestro of the Cliffs of Hong is now the Realized Man of Green City;[111] his grave is in Guzang county in Wuyi."[112]

111. Green City is the name of a mountain in Sichuan, fifth of the Ten Great Grotto Heavens of Taoism.
112. In Gansu.

[9]

Five Dynasties
(907–960)

Taoist Advice

Zhang Jianming

Zhang Jianming traveled north of the Yellow River for Confucian studies when he was young, then later left to become a Taoist priest. He mastered the doctrines of Lao-tzu and Chuang-tzu.

Emperor Gaozu of the Jin dynasty [r. 936–942] summoned him for an audience and asked, "Can Taoism be used to govern a country?" He replied, "The Way is a word for the essence of all things; if you get the last word, the ultimate statement, you can rule the world while at leisure in your bedroom." The emperor considered that advice great and invited him into the inner palace to lecture on the *Tao Te Ching*, honoring him as his teacher.

Hearing the drum announcing the hour in the palace, Jianming said, "Does Your Majesty hear the drum? It has only one note. None of the five notes and twelve semitones is in the drum, yet it is the drum that harmonizes them. Unity is the basis of myriad things; whoever can maintain unity can govern the world." The emperor approved of him even more and gave him the title Maestro Penetrating Mysteries.

Taoist Culture

Zheng Ao

Zheng Ao was styled Yansou. He was a man of Huazhou.[1] He was clever at literature and rhetoric and was nominated for *advanced*

---

1. In Henan.

scholar during the reign of Emperor Zhaozong of the Tang dynasty [r. 889–904], but he didn't pass the examination.

Seeing the world in chaos, he made a clean break and went away, going to Few Houses Mountain to become a Taoist priest. Hearing that on Huashan five globules of pine resin had seeped into the earth and over the course of a thousand years had turned into medicine that could eliminate the three parasites,[2] he moved his dwelling to Huayin to search for this.

He was good friends with the Taoist priests Li Daoyin and Luo Yinzhi. Ao planted fields, Yinzhi supported himself by selling herbs, and Daoyin had an art of fishing, hooking without baiting. He could also turn stones into gold; Ao once tested to see if that was true, but he didn't ask for any. The world called them the Three Lofty Gentlemen.

The regional commander Liu Ning sent him valuable goods, but he accepted nothing. Emperor Mingzong of [Latter] Tang [r. 926–934] summoned him to be an aide for picking up slips, responsible for pointing out imperial errors, and Emperor Gaozong of Jin [r. 936–941] summoned him to be grand master of remonstrance, but he did not comply with either. He was given the honorific appellation Meandering Maestro.

He died in 939 at the age of seventy-four.

Ao enjoyed drinking wine and playing chess. The poetry and prose he composed, written on gauze silk, were passed down in the world as prized curios. Some drew pictures of him on the walls of their houses to honor him in effigy. However remote his tracks, the more prominent his name, unlike the man at Stone Gate and the bamboo carrier.[3]

Taoist Disposition

LUQIU FANGYUAN

Luqiu Fangyuan was styled Dafang. He was a man of Susong in Shuzhou.[4] As a boy he was intelligent and eloquent; he studied the

2. Taoist medical theory envisions causes of decay and death as parasites in the three energy fields in the body.

3. The man at Stone Gate and the bamboo carrier are references to two recluses encountered by Confucius's disciple Zilu, as recorded in *Lunyu* 14:41 and 18:7, who are not otherwise named or identified.

4. In Anhui.

I Ching with Chen Xuanwu of Mount Lu and inquired into the great meaning from Zuo Xuanze of Xianglin. Zuo considered him extraordinary.

Later he moved to the Peak of the Realized in Hiding on Immortals' Capital Mountain, where he practiced transmundane arts following Liu Chujing[5] while not neglecting to read the many books of the philosophers and historians. He once said of himself, "Ge Hong and Tao Hongjing are my teachers and companions."[6] He wrote an exposition of the *Scripture on Great Peace* in thirty chapters, thoroughly elucidating its key essentials.

In 893 Qian Liu visited him in Great Cleansing Cave in Yuhang[7] and built a structure to house him. Qian reported Fangyuan's conduct and work to the emperor, and Zhaozong [r. 889–904] repeatedly tried to recruit him. Fangyuan figured from the signs of the heavens that China was going to be laid waste, the fortunes of the Tang dynasty were going to change, and even the likes of [ancient savants] Yuan and Qi[8] wouldn't come out of the mountain forests, so he never rose to the imperial summons. The emperor then sent down a decree praising him as extraordinary and bestowed on him a robe of rank and the titles Great Teacher of Subtle Being and Maestro of Mystic Accord.

Henceforth stories of the miracles of the realized were openly heard in Wu and Chu, and Fangyuan's disciples numbered more than two hundred. Cheng Zixiao of Guangping, who answered an invitation to the Qin palace; Nie Shidao of Xin-an, who carried on the teaching in the state of Wu; Hu Qianguang of Anding; and Kong Zonglu of the state of Lu all attained his mysteries.

On the fourteenth day of the second month of 902, he took a bath, then passed away sitting up straight. He was interred in the White Deer Grotto of Great Cleansing Mountain. King Xiao of Qianwu dreamed he visited, riding on a crane, to say farewell.

---

5. Liu Chujing was known for expertise in breathing exercises.
6. Ge Hong, compiler of *Legends of Spiritual Immortals* and author of *The Simpleton*, and Tao Hongjing the Recluse, master of Maoshan and compiler/author of *Declarations of the Realized*.
7. In Zhejiang.
8. Two of the oft-mentioned Four Elders.

NIE SHIDAO

Nie Shidao was styled Ziwei. He was a man of She in Xin-an.[9] He was exceptionally enlightened by nature, genuine and honest, deferential and discreet in speech and conduct. He was known for filial piety because of the way he took care of his parents.

Apprenticing himself to Luqiu Dafang, he went to the mountains east of the county and built a house on Governance Mountain. Once when he was reading esoteric traditions, he saw a formula for ingesting pine sap. Going into Hundred Fathom Mountain to collect pine sap, he met the realized men Cai, father and son,[10] and the realized man Peng.[11] He met the three immortals as soon as he went into the mountain, where one day and night was more than a month in the human world. This was actually determined by his diligent practice; Shidao himself was deeply moved by this rarity.

Whenever he gathered firewood and harvested herbs in the forest, a tiger and a leopard would follow him docilely. Sometimes he would load kindling and herbs on their backs and send them home. In the mountains near She, wild beasts didn't hurt people, all because of Shidao's ability to influence them.

His mother asked Shidao what benefit he got from traveling to study, and he told her all about those phenomena. Joyfully she said, "You take care of me with filial piety, and I ask about the Way—how lucky I am to be your mother!" This seems to have been a product of felicitous conduct in the past.

He went out to travel to Mount Heng and Mount Jiuyi and tried to find the realized man Mei and Attendant Gentleman Xiao on Jade Box Mountain. Mei was Mei Fu,[12] commandant of Nanchang, and Xiao was Ziyun, styled Jingqiao, a nobleman of Liang, who as governor of Dongyang fled into the mountains with his whole family to escape

---

9. In Anhui.
10. The Cai family is said to have received a visitation by the spiritual immortals Wang Yuan and the immortal lady Ma Gu in the second century C.E., hundreds of years before Nie Shidao lived.
11. There is a nostrum named after this figure, called Realized Man Peng's Life-Prolonging Pill, which is supposed to help the heart, produce blood, increase virility, darken the hair, make the skin lustrous, restore youth, and lengthen life.
12. First century B.C.E.

the rebellion of Houjing [in 548]. Both masters attained the Way on this mountain.

One day he wandered over to Fragrant Wood Pit [branching off Jade Box Mountain], where he happened to meet Xie Tongxiu,[13] who said of himself that he had originally lived on Mount Heng in seclusion with Peng and Cai. Xie led him back to his dwelling place and gave him a writing on silk. Then Shidao returned to Governance Mountain for more than thirty years. Every time he'd light incense and perform his practices, he would pay respects to images of the realized ones Peng, Cai, and Xie.

When the founder of Wu[14] took control of Jiangsu in 892, he heard of Nie Shidao, summoned him to Guangling, and built the Sanctuary of the Mystic Foundation as a residence for him, bestowing on him the honorific appellation Great Wandering Guide, Mentor of Governance Mountain. He lived in Guangling for another thirty years and had more than five hundred disciples.

After that he passed away in concealment, missed to a degree incomparable in his time. But a crane was repeatedly seen in the clouds over Governance Mountain, which villagers and relatives in She took to be Shidao returning to his native place, like Lingwei returning to Flower Front.[15]

An imperial decree of praise and entitlement says, "Consulting the classical standards of bestowal, bound to ancient norms, as a declaration has its reason, why should one not cite it? The late Nie Shidao, the Great Wandering Guide, Mentor of Governance Mountain, Taoist exemplar for the jurisdictions of Huai, Zhe, Xuan, and She, a great worthy who performed religious rites for the state and was granted a purple robe of honor, understood the principles of mysticism early on

13. A Taoist priest (757–855).

14. Yang Xingmi (d. 905), a regional inspector and military governor under the Tang dynasty, named prince of Wu in the last days of the Tang regime, established the state of Wu, one of the short-lived regimes in tenth-century southern China known as the Ten States. This period, between the fall of the Tang and the rise of the Song, is known as the period of the Five Dynasties and Ten States.

15. This alludes to a story about a legendary immortal named Ding Lingwei, who appeared as a white crane alighting atop a city gate pillar called Flower Front. When a youth tried to shoot the crane, it took wing, briefly circled the pillar, and identified itself as Ding Lingwei returning home after a thousand years; recommending the study of immortality, the crane then flew off into the sky.

and attained accord with the ways of the realized while still young;
outstanding as a wild crane, he was independent as a solitary cloud.

"In the past when the founder of Wu first established his base, he
already had Shidao carry out religious rites, so by the time the founding work was done and governance of the state was established, Shidao was already revered. His reflective words and plain conduct truly
capped the mystics.

"Although it has been some time since his ascent, the fine reputation he left has grown even greater in the world. Moreover, the religious schools have submitted requests, and the imperial assistants
have presented statements, so it shall be announced to the mystic
community that since Shidao has returned to his native place, here he
is to be awarded a high rank, given an honorable status, in order to
demonstrate approval and gratitude, hoping to bring to light his past
conduct. He is to be granted the title Maestro of Governance, Honorary Grand Master of the Silver and Blue Order, Chief Minister of
Court for State Ceremonial."

SONG DYNASTY
(960–1278)

Taoist Character

CHEN BO

Chen Bo was styled Tunan. He was a man of Xiaojun.[1] When he was small he was playing by the Guo River when a maid took him to her breast and nursed him, saying, "I'll make you forever free of desire."

His brilliance was beyond others. He was nominated for *advanced scholar* in the Changxing era [930–933] of the [Later] Tang dynasty but didn't pass the examination. He went into seclusion on Mount Wudang, where he abstained from grain and trained his breath. He composed a collection of eighty-one poems, called *Pointing to the Mystery*. Emperor Mingzong of the Later Tang dynasty [r. 926–934] entitled him Independent Scholar of Purity and Emptiness. Shortly he moved to Cloud Terrace Monastery on Huashan, where he kept his door shut and lay for months on end without rising.

Emperor Shizong of the Later Zhou dynasty [r. 944–949] summoned him to the palace to test his genuineness. In 960 Chen Bo was about to enter the eastern capital riding a white mule when he heard that Taizu of Song had assumed the throne; laughing aloud, he said, "The land is stabilized!"

Emperor Taizong [of the Song dynasty, r. 976–997] summoned him in his time, but Tunan wrote a refusal, saying, "My nature is like a monkey or a bird, and my mind is like dead ashes. I do not understand the shallow and deep of humanity and righteousness, so how can I know the conduct of ritual behavior? I make clothing of dead lotus leaves and a hat of sloughed-off bamboo sheaths; my body has

---

1. In Anhui.

abundant hair, my feet have no straw sandals. Were I to come to court, I'd give Your Majesty a laugh."

The emperor then sent a palace receptionist to be sure to rouse him, and presented a poem:

> Having emerged from the white clouds before the
>   previous court,
> Since then there has been no news;
> Now if you'll agree to obey the imperial summons,
> We'll give the whole Three Peaks of Huashan to you.

Tunan could no longer refuse to go to the palace, so he showed up in the manner of a guest, with a Huayang turban on his head, wearing straw sandals, a feather robe, and a hanging sash. He was given the honorific appellation Maestro of the Imperceptible and Invisible and sent to the Secretariat. A commissioner told the executive minister Song Qi and others, "Bo only takes care of himself and has no interest in power or profit. He has been on Huashan for forty years now and is nearly one hundred years old. Because the land is at peace, he has shown up at court. Be considerate of him."

Qi and the others then inquired about the path of practical cultivation. He replied, "The sage above has a sundial indicating the proper times for ruler and ministers to combine their virtues to plan policy; what can devotional practices add to this?"

Grandees would go daily asking for good advice; he replied to all of them, "Don't be attached to ease, don't revisit satisfactions." Those who were knowledgeable approved of this.

Tunan was conversant with all the classics, but he was most expert in *I Ching* study, which he transmitted to his disciple Mu Xiu, who transmitted it to Li Zhicai, who transmitted it to Professor Kangjie, Shao Yong.[2] He also transmitted *Diagram of the Absolute* to Zhong Fang, who transmitted it to Mu Xiu, who transmitted it to Professor Lianxi, Zhou Moshu.[3]

---

2. Shao Yong (1011–1077), a very famous scholar, is considered one of the founding fathers of neo-Confucian idealism.

3. That is, Zhou Dunyi (1017–1073), who, like Shao Yong, was considered a founding father of neo-Confucian idealism, which integrates Taoist metaphysics and Buddhist meditation into Confucian moralism.

Tunan made predictions based on past calculations that subsequently proved to be so; his perceptive understanding of the human condition was legendary. When Taizu[4] was still living in obscurity, he roamed the markets of Chang'an with Zhao Zhongxian. Meeting him on the street, Tunan said, "Shall we have a drink?" Taizu said, "Let's bring Scholar Zhao along." Tunan gave him a hard look and said, "Very well, then." When they got to the tavern, Zhongxian, who was suffering from numbness in his foot, immediately sat down to the right. Tunan scolded him, "Does one small star in the Lilac Fence constellation[5] dare raise its position?" And with that he pulled him down off the seat.

When Tunan was summoned by the emperor Taizong, the emperor had him see King Shou [the emperor's third son]. Tunan went as far as the gate, then came back and said, "The king's establishment has a full staff of servants; why should I see the king?" Because of this Taizong put his confidence in King Shou as his designated successor, who became the emperor Zhenzong.

In 989 he foresaw his death. He had an announcement delivered to the emperor saying, "Destiny has an end; one cannot cling even to an era of a sage." He had his disciple Jia Desheng excavate a stone crypt in Zhang Chao Valley;[6] when the crypt was done, he passed on. Five-hued clouds covered the mountain valley for a month without dispersing.

A Taoist Scholar

WANG ZHAOSU

Wang Zhaosu was a man of Suanzao.[7] He studied the Way early in life and was particularly expert in the I Ching. He once said, "Earth is the symbol of the tenth month. In the tenth month, pure yin manages things, but there is still yang energy inside; that is why greens and wheat grow first. Even at the end of the Earth symbol there is still the image of dragons battling; since the dragon is yang, we know that there

---

4. Founder of the Song dynasty, r. 960–976. *Living in obscurity* means this incident took place before he became emperor.
5. The throne of the god of the sky.
6. On Huashan.
7. In Henan.

is no way yang can be stripped away completely. That is because yin and yang alternate in the use of firmness and flexibility, changing anew every day, sustaining regeneration of life without end."

He was deeply into the Way. Local people respected his conduct so much that when they had complaints they'd resort to him for decisions instead of going to the government offices.

In 969 he was summoned by the emperor to lecture on the *I Ching*. After a month he sought to return. He was specially granted the title of Doctor of the National University and sent off courteously, being already advanced in age by that time.

He died when he was more than ninety years old. His neck shrunk into his midsection, and people said he was capable of turtle breathing.[8]

Taoist Advice

ZHENG YIN

Zheng Yin was styled Xizhen. He was a man of Changshan.[9] He mastered both esoteric and exoteric studies.

When Taizu conquered the great plain, he visited Zheng's abode. Xizhen was eighty years old at the time, but he appeared very young. Taizu asked him about his way of nurturing life. He replied, "For me, nurturing life is meditation and training the breathing, that's all; it's different for emperors and kings. Lao-tzu says, 'I do nothing and the people are spontaneously civilized; I am clear and calm and the people are spontaneously upright.' No contrivance, no desire, stabilizing the spirit in universal harmony—the Yellow Emperor and King Yao had charge of the nation for a hundred years because they attained this Way."

The emperor was delighted. This man seems to have been rather like Sun Simiao.[10]

---

8. On turtle breathing, see *Yunji qiqian* in *Daozang jiyao*, vol. 20, p. 8685. Compare the representation in *Xianshu biku* II, p. 26.
9. In Hebei.
10. A famous physician.

ZHANG WUMENG

Zhang Wumeng was styled Lingyin. He was a man of Zhouzhi in Fengxiang.[11] He was an informal associate of Zhong Fang[12] and Liu Haichan.[13] Journeying to Red City[14] on Mount Tiantai, he made a hut on the Coral Terrace. He once said, "Unity is the function of the Way. Essentially it has no location, no substance, no function, no contrivance; without contrivance there is nothing it doesn't do. Even insects have the nature of the Way. Those who attain the Way are all transformed: on a small scale, dung beetles transform into cicadas; on a larger scale, humans can transform into immortals."

Here he observed the changes of sky and earth, the flourishing and fading of plants and trees, the contraction and expansion of wind and clouds, the revolution of the sun and moon, the mutual stimulation of water and fire, the patterns of interaction of yin and yang. He wrote *Returning to the Origin* in one hundred chapters.

Emperor Zhenzong [r. 998–1022] summoned him for a meeting and asked him about the teaching of eternal life. He answered, "Living in the mountains, I just read the *I Ching* and *Lao-tzu*, that's all. I don't know anything else." So the emperor had him lecture on the *I Ching*, whereupon he explained the symbol Humility. The emperor said, "Why only expound Humility?" He replied, "At a time of great possession, it should be preserved by humility."[15] The emperor deeply agreed with this.

The emperor also had him lecture on *Returning to the Origin*. He

---

11. In Shaanxi.

12. Zhong Fang (955–1015) lived on Mount Zhongnan for thirty years, teaching privately. He was a transmitter of esoteric *I Ching* lore seminal in the foundation of neo-Confucian idealism.

13. Liu Haichan is considered the fourth patriarch of the northern school of Complete Reality (Quanzhen) Taoism, notice of which is otherwise generally excluded from this collection.

14. Sixth of the Ten Great Grotto Heavens of Taoism.

15. In the traditional order of the *I Ching* symbols, the sign for Humility (no. 15) follows the sign for Great Possession (no. 14). The influential commentary of the eleventh-century neo-Confucian Cheng Yi says, "Those whose possessions are great should not get puffed up with pride; so the next symbol after Great Possession is Humility." In this instance, reference to *great possession* is understood to allude to the position of the emperor.

said, "The nation is just like the mind. When there is no contrivance in the mind, then the mood is peaceful; when the mood is peaceful, myriad jewels crystallize. When there is contrivance in the mind, the mood is disturbed, and when the mood is disturbed, flowers fall. This is the general outline of returning to the source."

Emperor Zhenzong admired him and considered him extraordinary. He presented him with a rank and entitled him a court gentleman, but he refused to accept and insistently pleaded to be allowed to return to the mountains. Later he died in Jinling, at the age of ninety-nine. Chen Jingyuan, Master of the Blue Sky,[16] was his disciple.

LIU LIE

Liu Lie was a man of Jiujiang. He took a liking to the Way as a boy. Meeting an unusual person who had attained the Way during the Lianlong era [960–963], he built a hut on Mount Lu and privately practiced his path, calling himself the Man of the Empty Valley.

In the past there had been someone named Tan Jingsheng who composed *A Book of Transformation*.[17] Lie summarized its essential points in these terms: "The sky is vast yet has bounds; the emperor is great yet has an abode. Finding the gateway to immense energy is the means of absorbing its root; knowing the container of the elemental spirit is the means of hiding its light. Like an oyster guarding inside and a rock concealing within, in storage it is the elemental vitality; in action it is myriad spirits. Contained, it is great unity; released, it is great purity. The main sources are *Lao-tzu, Chuang-tzu,* and the *Yellow Court*."

He used to say, "Myriad things cannot influence the nature of those who learn the Way; they are single-minded, profoundly calm, and free from cogitation. Guiding their energy according to the time, they are physically comfortable. Embracing unadulterated purity, cultivating the great mystery, after that they do not enter into their impulses. So if you know how to preserve spirit, produce energy, and restore vitality, what can you not attain!"

16. Some of Chen's commentary on the *Tao Te Ching* is cited in *The Essential Tao* by Thomas Cleary (1991), pp. 131–60.

17. For extracts from this work, see *Vitality, Energy, Spirit* (Thomas Cleary, 1991), pp. 151–55.

ZHANG QIANXIAO

Zhang Qianxiao was the twenty-fourth-generation descendant of the Celestial Teacher of the Han dynasty.[18] In the year 1030 he was summoned to the imperial palace, where Emperor Renzong asked him about ascension in broad daylight. He replied, "This is of no help to governance and education. If Your Majesty can return to the plainness of old and practice simplicity, then your will and thought shall be pure and clear, your spirit and mood shall be wholesome and mellow. Why be concerned with ascension?" The emperor appreciated this and gave him the honorific name Teacher of Clarifying the Elemental.

Taoist Disposition

FU LIN

Fu Lin was a man of Qingzhou.[19] When he was young he was a fellow student of Zhang Zhongding.[20] After Zhongding had reached a high rank, he sought Fu Lin for thirty years but couldn't find him. Once he even wrote a poem to express how much he missed him. In his later years, when he was governor of Wanling, someone in rustic clothing riding a donkey knocked at the gate of his mansion and shouted, "Tell the secretary that Fu Lin of Qinqzhou has arrived."

The doorkeeper ran to deliver the message. Zhongding said angrily, "Maestro Fu is a world-famous scholar; who are you, daring to invoke a distinguished name?"

Lin laughed and said, "It's been a lifetime since I last saw you, and I'm still this naive; how should I have known I existed in the context of the world?"

Zhongding asked, "Why have you come out of your long-standing seclusion now?"

He said, "You're about to leave, so I came to inform you, that's all."

Zhongding said, "I know it myself."

18. That is, Zhang Ling, or Zhang Daoling.
19. In Shandong.
20. Zhang Ying served as a provincial governor and, in the central government, as auxiliary academician of the Bureau of Military Affairs and secretary of the Ministry of Personnel. The name Zhongding is his honorific posthumous name, indicating recognition for distinguished service to the state.

He said, "If you know, what more is there to say?" So he left, not saying where he was going. A month later, Zhongding died.

Taoist Silence

Shuai Zilian

Shuai Zilian was a farmer of Mount Heng. He was uneducated, simple, and intractable, and people called him Shuai the Ox. In later life he entered Southern Peak Monastery and became a Taoist priest.

Seven *li* southwest of the monastery was the Cloister of the Purple Void, which had been the altar of Madame Wei[21] in the past. Because it was a ruin, no Taoist priests wanted to live there, except for Zilian, who alone enjoyed living there. He maintained a strict silence, and no one observed his activities.

Now then, he was quite fond of wine, and time and again he'd lie drunk in the mountain forest, oblivious even to wind and rain. Tigers and wolves passed right by him without doing him any harm. Then when Wang Gongu, attendant gentleman of the Ministry of Rites, became governor of Changsha, he visited the altar of Madame Wei while carrying out an imperial order to offer prayers on Mount Heng. Zilian was lying drunk at the time, unable to get up. He looked straight at the governor and said, "I love wine but can't always get it, so when I do I get drunk straightaway." The officers were angry at this, but Governor Wang perceived how extraordinary he was and had him carried back. For more than a month he remained alone, saying nothing, so the governor returned him to the mountains, saying, "The honored master hides his light, illumined within; he's incomprehensible to me. He should be presented with poetry."

After the governor had forgotten about this, one day while he was taking a nap he dreamed Zilian came asking for the poetry. He then composed two four-line verses, printed them, and had them put in the cloister. The Taoist priests said in surprise, "How did Shuai the Ox get these?"

On the twenty-seventh day of the sixth month of 980, Shuai suddenly told someone in the monastery, "I'm going to go somewhere; the

21. For Madame Wei (Wei Huacun), see the story of Yang Xi.

cloister shouldn't be vacant, so you should send someone to succeed me soon." Even more surprised, the congregation said, "The weather is so hot, where is Shuai the Ox going?" Confused, they looked in on him and saw he was dead. Now they really marveled at him, exclaiming, "Shuai the Ox knew the day of his death!" Then they buried him on the mountainside.

Before long, as Shouzheng, a Buddhist monk of South Terrace Temple, was returning from the eastern capital, he ran into Zilian outside Nanxun Gate, his spirit and mood clear and buoyant. Shouzheng asked him why he'd left the mountain. Laughing, he said, "Just a leisure excursion, that's all," and entrusted him with a letter for the people on the mountain. When Shouzheng got back, he found out Zilian had died; opening the letter, he saw it was the date of his death. They opened the grave and found nothing but a staff and shoes.

Taoist Arts

ZHAO JI

Zhao Ji was a man of Daizhou.[22] After he had attained the Way, he went around begging in the streets of Gao'an,[23] so he was considered unclean.

In 1080, Su Zhe Ziyou[24] was banished to Gao'an. Ji unexpectedly crossed Ziyou's path and said, "I know you like the Way, but you do not yet know the essentials. As yang does not descend and yin does not rise, you're fleshy and flabby, your face is red and blotchy. I'd advise you to draw water and wash your whole body; in ten days your ailments will disappear. If you are not lazy, transcending the world is possible." Ziyou followed his advice, and it worked.

Another day he asked about nurturing nature. Ji told him, "Do you ever dream? When you're dreaming, do you still have knowledge of living and dying, or sorrow and happiness?"

He said, "This can't be constant."

22. In Shanxi.
23. In Jiangxi.
24. Su Zhe was a famous scholar, writer, and statesman. Ziyou was his style. He was the younger brother of Su Shi, one of the most famous poets in Chinese history. Deeply involved in political controversies of the time, Su Zhe experienced many ups and downs in his career.

Ji laughed and said, "If there is a difference between dreaming and waking, then your nature isn't whole."

Stunned, Ziyou marveled at him, realizing he was truly one who had the Way.

Ji said of himself that he had been in Guangling in the past, where a fellow student, Jiang Sheng, had poisoned his eyes so they clouded. However, in time he was able to get rid of the clouding, and his eyes became clear as the sky.

The bones above his waist were like a turtle, below his heart like a spade. The bones met in between but did not join, like fingers. At the time he was a 127 years old.

Later he came to the commandery of Xingguo,[25] where the prefect Yang Hui Yuansu got him to stay. He had not been there long before the mule he kept kicked him and he died. Yuansu had him buried.

In 1086 a Buddhist monk from Shu, Fazhen, came to see the elder Mr. Su[26] at the eastern capital. He said, "I saw a beggar at a tavern in Yun-an who said his name was Zhao and that he had recently come to know Mr. Su was in Huangzhou and requested me to ask after you." When Ziyou heard about this, he was surprised and asked what the beggar looked like; then he realized it was Ji. The son of the prefect of the commandery of Xingguo, one Zhu Yanbo, was present at the time; he went home and told his father, who opened the crypt. There were only a staff and two shinbones there, that's all. What Taoist books call the lowest grade of liberation from the corpse leaves behind a bone of the foot—could this be what that refers to?

Taoist Advice

LI HAO

Li Hao was a man of Jianzhou.[27] He was skilled at charms. When Chen Shugu[28] was governing Chenzhou,[29] there were a lot of ghosts haunting the office building. So the building was vacated and Hao was brought in; then the ghosts stopped. Su Zhe questioned him closely,

25. In Jiangxi.
26. That is, Su Shi (also known as Su Dongpo).
27. In Sichuan.
28. Lived from 1017 to 1080.
29. In Henan.

saying, "How could you do that?" Hao replied, "He has a lot of desire, so the ghosts were contemptuous of him. I gave up desire long ago. That's all there is to it."

From time to time he was asked about how to nurture life. He would reply, "People are born with the five elemental forces of heaven and earth, equivalent to heaven and earth; the five elemental forces operate in heaven and earth without end, yet human life is no more than a hundred years, simply because of being self-destructive. That is, while alive we recognize a distinction between things and self; inside is self, outside are things. As long as the sense of things and self is not forgotten in the mind, self and things are divided, so the energies of the five elemental forces one receives are disconnected from the five elemental forces at large; depending on how much they receive, individuals use up what they have and stop, so some live long and some die young. Now, if you genuinely forget the difference between things and self, causing this body to commune with heaven and earth as one, then the energies of the five elemental forces will circulate inside and outside without exhaustion. Then how could anyone fail to live long!"

Taoist Culture

ZHU ZIYING

Zhu Ziying was styled Lingzhi. He was a man of Red Sun Village on Juqu [Maoshan]. He was born in 976. At the age of eight or nine he followed the herder Guo Cancan and could attract cranes by playing the flute. His parents considered this inauspicious, and they abandoned him.

Then he followed Zhu Yuanji of Maoshan and donned the robe of a Taoist priest. At that time, in 988, he was twelve years old.

Next he stayed on the peak of Piled Gold Mountain [of Maoshan] with the enlightened realized man Zhang the Alchemist, trying a technique of avoiding grain. People began to approach him, so in time he wanted to go far away.

Coming to Xiangyang,[30] he met a strange man, Iron Legs Chen, who went with him to Green City Mountain.[31] Then he went back to

30. In Hubei.
31. In Sichuan.

his native place and edited the old canon at the Sanctuary of Great Purity.

Meeting the Boy of the Planet Mercury, Immortal Boy Wu, whose name was Baoyi, he accompanied him to Hezhongfu.[32] He said this trip was already equivalent to a refinement of the body in total yin,[33] and his behavior miraculously changed.

In 1004 he was made the twenty-third-generation heir of the scriptures and charts of Maoshan. Emperor Zhenzong sent a commissioner to pray for progeny on the mountain, and [the emperor's son and successor] Renzong was born the following year. The facts are in the *History of Song*.

In obedience to a directive, Ziying became abbot of the Sanctuary of Shining Reflection of Jadelike Purity. The emperor ordered the construction of two monasteries, one called Foundation of the Creative and the other Celestial Sage, and granted him the title Teacher of the Nation. The empress Mingxiao, who received the summary teachings of the *Great Grotto Scripture of Realization*,[34] gave him another title, Master of Observing the Subtle.

Returning to the mountains, he found letters Baoyi had sent from Shu warning him about letting his name become prominent and disclosing the celestial workings. The maestro wept streams of tears at this. None of his disciples could fathom why.

In the eleventh month of 1029 he passed away sitting at the Foundation of the Creative Monastery, holding in his hand the jade scepter bestowed on him as a token; perspiration covered his body, and there were congealed drops on his brow, an example of the highest kind of liberation from the corpse.[35]

---

32. In Shanxi.
33. This refers to a state of temporary death.
34. See *Yunji qiqian* in *Daozang jiyao*, vol. 19, pp. 8449 et passim.
35. Heavy perspiration like this can be evidence of a heart attack or congestive heart failure. While this man lived to no great age for a Taoist adept, he was not too young for a heart attack, and his story suggests a history of exceptional stress, like some early Maoshan masters. Even though a heart attack would not necessarily be fatal, expertise in the practice of projecting the spirit should enable one to leave the body painlessly and permanently in case of such an event. Hence the term *liberation from the corpse.*

Taoist Character

LIU HUNKANG

Liu Hunkang was a man of Jinling. In 1060 he took examinations in the scriptures and became a Taoist priest. One night he dreamed that a spirit told him, "If you want to study the Way, you must choose a distinguished mountain." Always troubled by the absence of good teachers in those times, he used to climb up to altars with his hair loose, taking nature for his religion. Eventually he heard that Religious Master Mao of Maoshan had the Way.

Mao took one look at him and passed on to him the scriptures and charts. He took up residence in a hermitage on Piled Gold Peak of Maoshan.

One day three Taoists came to his hermitage. Pointing to the east corner of the hermitage, one said, "You live here, embrace spirit and keep centered, while your generosity extends to others; you would have nothing to be ashamed of in front of the ancients." Another looked at his forehead and said, "This is the place of nondoing, valued on the Way. It shouldn't have any blemish." Then he rubbed it with his hand. The next day a scar had disappeared.

In 1086 Emperor Zhezong heard of him and summoned him as an eminent Taoist, ordering him to dwell in the Sanctuary of Accumulated Blessings of the Highest Purity Path. In 1097 the emperor decreed that the Hermitage of the Hidden Spirit where he had lived in Jiangningfu be made the Monastery of Accord with the Origin, and in a separate decree ordered that the religious establishment of the Mountain of the Three Maos, Dragon and Tiger Mountain[36] of Xinzhou, and Gezao Mountain[37] in the Linjiang commandery be made the Three Mountains for scriptures and charts.[38]

---

36. In Jiangxi, a principal center of the cult of the Celestial Masters. There are two sectarian histories of this mountain center, called *Longhushan zhi*, or *Annals of Dragon and Tiger Mountain*, one from the Yuan dynasty (1278–1348) and one from the Qing dynasty (1644–1912).

37. In Jiangxi, this mountain was the original center of the Spiritual Jewel (Lingbao) cult and one of the thirty-three rich earths (*fudi*) of Taoist topography.

38. This alludes to the amalgamation of the Celestial Master, Maoshan, and Spiritual Jewel cults in the True Unity denomination of Taoism.

Emperor Huizong enlarged the monastery; augmented its name to Sanctuary of Accord with the Origin, Security for the Multitude; and presented many precious gifts, such as a jade seal of the Lord of the City of Nine Elderly Immortals, a jade cup engraved with clouds and lightning, the light-thunder sword, and imperial calligraphy and paintings.

The maestro repeatedly announced impending disasters and deviations, but while the emperor admired him, he was unable to make use of his advice.

In 1108 the emperor again called him out of the mountains. A group of deer blocked the road; one of the deer got hit by the carriage and died. They buried it on the left side of the road. Before this, a crane that he kept flew away on hearing the summons. The maestro said, "The crane left, a deer died—it looks like I'll never return."

In the fourth month he reached the capital and was lodged in a newly constructed cloister at the Monastery of Accord with the Origin. That night he dreamed that the Lord of Heaven summoned him. The next day the emperor visited, and he presented the *Scripture of the Great Grotto* he recited. On the seventeenth day of the month he suddenly passed away. He was seventy-two years old.

The emperor ordered the construction of the Monastery of Concealing the Real at the site of his tomb and added titles, including Maestro of Subtle Deep Harmony of the Monastery of Preserving the Real, bestowing on him the rank of Superior Grand Master of the Palace, with the posthumous name Calm and Unified.

Taoist Advice

Cha Jingzhi

Cha Jingzhi was styled Qingyuan. He was a man of Jinling. His father took him to Maoshan; Master Liu, seeing him, considered him extraordinary and said, "Someday this boy will be a teacher of men and gods."[39] He jumped for joy and vowed never to return home. Eventually he became one of the inner circle of disciples.

---

39. *Teacher of men and gods* is one of the ten major epithets of a buddha, used as a term of highest praise.

During the Yuanyou era [1086–1093] he went along with Master Liu to the imperial court. The senior master was directed to dwell at the Sanctuary of Stored Blessings, while this master [Cha] was assigned to manage the affairs of the Sanctuary of Accord with the Origin.

On the third day of the seventh month of 1183, he called his disciples and said, "This year I'm forty-six years old. In the past my former teacher predicted I wouldn't live any longer than this because of excessive indulgence in the favors of the imperial court." He then had a final testament prepared and took up a brush and personally wrote a note at the end of the statement, saying, "Your Majesty has been granted sagacity by heaven; no emperor or king since ancient times has respected the Way and honored virtue more. However, remember that for emperors and kings the service of the Way is not the same as for subjects and commoners. One pronouncement or one action of the ruler in accord with the heart of heaven brings benefit everywhere. The five thousand words of Lao-tzu make a priority of getting rid of extravagance and violence, being kind and frugal—this is Your Majesty's guiding jewel, the bridge to the Way. I humbly pray that Your Majesty will purify his heart and minimize his desires in order to preserve the imperial person; be sparing of resources and frugal in expenditures in order to strengthen the root of the nation; listen to the loyal and the good in order to widen the routes of advice. The felicity of the land will be great!

"Stupid as I am, I certainly shouldn't be setting forth a speech at the risk of death, but in reality I'm being mindful of the gravity of the charge entrusted to me by my late teacher, who used to direct me to make a priority of being thorough in loyalty to requiting the country. At this juncture, if I do not offer a single word to foster the emperor's virtue, then as a subject I would be disobeying heaven and turning my back on my teacher, carrying resentment to the underworld.

"Taking brush in hand, I set forth my feelings, humbly seeking to increase a sense of pity. Subject Jingzhi, repeating his words."

After putting his seal on the document, he passed away.

This was reported to the emperor. Huizong lamented unceasingly. He had the testament entrusted to the Monastery of Concealing the Real and carved in stone on Maoshan.

Taoist Influence

XU SHOUXIN

Xu Shouxin was a man of Hailing.[40] He was a menial worker at the Monastery of Celestial Celebration. He wore ragged clothes of plain cloth and either wore rope sandals or went barefoot. He did nothing all day but sweep and clean, but he also recited the *Scripture on Liberating Humanity*[41] continuously.

There was a Taoist priest, Xu Yuanji, who came from somewhere else, suffering from a severe case of leprosy. He was shunned by the whole congregation, who quarantined him in a reed hut behind the monastery. Shouxin alone attended to him, respectfully. Then when Yuanji died, Shouxin went begging for cash to take up a collection for him, and after having him buried he went back to the reed hut and mourned for three days. When he came out he acted insane; quite a few extraordinary phenomena were attributed to him, and people all considered him a wonder, calling him the Miraculous Old Man. Only then was it realized that he had gotten the Way from the leprous Taoist priest.

Henceforth many came from all quarters to ask him about calamity and fortune. When Emperor Zhezong was unwell, he sent incense to the Miraculous Old Man, who wrote back, "Good man." Before long, Huizong succeeded to the throne.

In 1102 the emperor summoned him, but he wouldn't go, so the emperor had him conveyed to the eastern capital by force. The emperor still couldn't keep him there, so he sent him back courteously. Then the emperor had Sanctuary of Eternal Life, Spring of Immortals built in Hailing and had him reside there.

In 1109 the emperor summoned him to the palace. On the seventeenth day of the fourth month, Shouxin heard that Master Liu of Maoshan had passed away at the Cloister of Accumulated Blessings; he said, "Master Liu has gone; I'm going too!" Then he passed away on the twentieth of the month. For this reason the emperor issued a decree containing the words, "Moved by sincerity, unusual people repeatedly arrive; passing away in full consciousness, they're the same

40. In Jiangsu.
41. This belongs to the Spiritual Jewel (Lingbao) corpus. See *Daozang jiyao*, vol. 2.

without prearrangement." Shouxin was given the title of Superior Grand Master of the Palace, in terms no different from the announcement for Master Liu.

Taoist Character

ZHANG JIXIAN

Zhang Jixian was the thirtieth-generation descendant of the Celestial Teacher of Han. He got his teaching at the age of nine. Profoundly silent, seldom speaking, he was thin and pale, with the appearance of a genuine celestial personage. Emperor Huizong sent a commissioner to summon him, and when he arrived the emperor entitled him Grand Master of the Blue Sky. The maestro was just thirteen years old and refused to accept.

In 1105 he was summoned again and ordered to put a stop to strange phenomena occurring at the salt fields of Jiezhou. He was extraordinarily effective and was given the honorific name Maestro of Emptiness and Serenity.

During the Zhenghe era [1111–1117] there was a tremendous internal disaster, and he was ordered to pray to get rid of it. On this occasion he submitted a statement on the ill omen of the red sheep and red horse; the words were cryptic [alluding to the coming years 1126 and 1127].

In 1126 the invaders withdrew and the imperial court again sent a commissioner to the governor of the county to go to the maestro's cottage to summon him, making sure to get him to go.

When the maestro came to Yuhang on the way, he appeared displeased, but no one could figure out why. Then they learned that foreigners had invaded again, plundering,[42] and he was called to court as soon as possible. When he got to the Monastery of Celestial Celebration in Sizhou, he passed away, sitting upright. He was thirty-six years old. This was actually in 1127.

---

42. In 1127 invading forces of the Jin dynasty of the north, ruled by Ruzhen people, captured the Chinese emperor and his father/predecessor, who had reigned for twenty-five years. This year marks the beginning of the so-called Southern Song, when the government of China finally moved south under the pressure of invasion and expansion of other powers into northern China.

Later the wayfarer Sa Shoujian encountered the maestro at Green City Mountain. Emperor Gaozong [r. 1127–1162] had an image of him installed in a cloister within the palace. His writings, *Song of the Great Way* and *Explanation of Mind*, were transmitted in the world.

Taoist Advice

LIU GAOSHANG

Liu Gaoshang was a man of Anding in Pinzhou.[43] His family had been farmers for generations. He stopped eating meat at the age of nine and afterward gradually stopped speaking. When asked about anything, he'd write the answer. His words seemed incomprehensible at first but turned out to be true. His family built a separate room for him to live in.

Eventually word got around, and people far and near considered him spiritual. Emperor Huizong sent three commissioners to go invite him, but he refused on the grounds of illness and did not obey the imperial command. The emperor gave him the honorific name Lofty Independent Scholar and built him a sanctuary to live in. His followers named it after him.

During the disturbance of 1126, foreign invaders saw Gaoshang. They all dismounted from their horses and bowed in unison. They did not dare enter his village.

Gaoshang used to have an adage, "People of the world kill their bodies with desire, kill their posterity with money, kill others with government, and kill the world with scholarship." [Another source has "Don't kill your body with desire, don't kill your posterity with money, don't kill others with government, don't kill the world with scholarship."] The knowledgeable of later generations considered this a memorable saying.

In composing a biography for him, Zhou Shaoyin[44] also expanded upon his adage and expounded it, considering that the discourse of

43. There were numerous places called Anding (which means "peaceful and stable") under various dynasties; Pinzhou was in Shandong.
44. Zhou Shaoyin was a scholar, poet, and civil servant of the Shaoxing era (1131–1162) of the Song dynasty.

this erudite of old on how the great realized people saved the drowning, revived the dead, and restored reality could never be attained by a commonplace wordsmith. The fact that the maestro, as the son of farmers, had never read books or studied with a teacher and yet had this adage might suggest he was one among the spiritual immortals, with deep knowledge of the Way. He was certainly different from those who labor over the years doing calisthenics and breathing exercises hoping to get their names on the register of immortals!

WANG DAOJIAN

Wang Daojian was a Taoist priest of Dragon and Tiger Mountain. During the Zhenghe era [1111–1117] he was summoned to the imperial palace, where emperor Huizong asked him about the art of training to extend the life span. He reported, "Purity and calm, without contrivance, were the means whereby the Yellow Emperor governed; having many desires and seeking immortality were the means by which Emperor Wu of Han nullified his achievements. Training is not a matter for an emperor."

At that time a critical edition of the Taoist canon was in progress, and the emperor decreed that Daojian be given the title Grand Master of the Elemental and a position on the editorial board at the Shrine for Concentrating the Spirit, to collaborate on the critical edition of the Taoist scriptures.

Emperor Huizong knew in advance that the country was going to have trouble and ordered Daojian to exorcise it. He reported, "Practicing virtue can cause the heavens to revolve; when it comes to exorcism, I dare not mislead the country." He strongly requested to be allowed to return to the mountains.

In the early 1130s Emperor Gaozong dispatched a commissioner to summon him again. One day earlier, Daojian had beaten the drum to assemble the whole congregation, then cited a verse with the lines, "Reply to the commissioner from the capital / Stop looking for the mountains on the sea."[45] By the time the commissioner arrived, Daojian had already passed away.

---

45. *The mountains on the sea* refers to so-called isles of immortality, here by implication to immortality itself.

Taoist Arts

Liu Yongguang

Liu Yongguang was a man of Guixi in Xinzhou. His face was unusual, like a person of antiquity, and dark. He reached manhood with no education. Traveling to Mount Heng, when he came to Lin'an county in Wuzhou, he met a Taoist on the road who introduced himself as Zhang Fuyuan and went along with him.

As they traveled, Yongguang carried Zhang's baggage, and when they stopped he cooked for Zhang. When they were putting up in Changsha, Zhang said to him, "You have served me diligently and thoroughly. Earlier, I was treating you contemptuously to see if you'd change, but you've become increasingly respectful. I'm going into Shu now; I have a book I'm giving to you. Keep it secret." Then he left.

When Yongguang opened the book and looked at it, he saw it was *Five Thunder Writings*.

During the late 1190s there was a drought in Quzhou. The prefectural governor Shen Zuoli dreamed one night that a black dragon lay coiled at the gate of Chenghuang Shrine. When he looked there in the morning, there was Yongguang lying drunk. Then he ordered him to pray for rain, and it rained. The prefectural authorities reported the incident, and when he prayed for rain again at court, it also rained then.

Yongguang was almost forty years old and had never been ordained as a Taoist priest. At this point he was given a hat and outfit in the imperial presence and presented the honorific title Master of Empty Serenity. Emperor Ningzong [r. 1195–1225] laid out imperial funds to renew and enlarge the Sanctuary of Higher Purity.

When Lizong assumed the throne [in 1225], he summoned Yongguang again. Yongguang told the envoy, "Go back and report to the emperor that to govern the land the five-thousand-character *Tao Te Ching* is sufficient. What can a rustic of the mountain forests add by coming?" In the end he passed away on Dragon and Tiger Mountain.

Some say that the Zhang Fuyuan whom he had met was the Celestial Teacher of Han.

SELECT BIBLIOGRAPHY

Chen Guofu. *Daozang Yuanliu kao.* Taibei: Xiangsheng Publishing Co., 1975.

Chen Yaoding et al., eds. *Daojia yangsheng shu.* Shanghai: Fudan University Press, 1992.

Chen Yongzheng, ed. in chief. *Zhongguo fangshu dacidian.* Guangzhou, China: Zhongshan University Press, 1991.

China Taoist Association. *Daojiaoshi ciliao.* Shanghai: Shanghai Ancient Texts Publishing Co., 1991.

Dai Yuanchang, comp., and Li Luoqiu, ed. *Daoxue cidian.* Taibei: Zhenshanmei Publishing Co., 1976.

———. *Xianxue cidian.* Taibei: Zhenshanmei Publishing Co., 1962.

Daoxuan. *Gaosengchuan erji.* Taibei: Taiwan Scripture Printing Center, 1970.

Du Jiexiang, ed. in chief. *Daojiao wenxian.* Taibai: Danqing Book Co., 1983.

Hong Jianlin, ed. *Daojia yangsheng biku.* Dalian, China: Dalian Publishing Co., 1991.

Huang Gongwei. *Daojiao yu xiudao biyi zhiyao.* Taibei: Xinwenfeng Publishing Co., 1982.

Huijiao. *Gaosengchuan.* Taibei: Taiwan Scripture Printing Center, 1973.

Li Shuhuan, comp. *Daojiao dacidian.* Hong Kong: Tiandaoshe Printing, 1980.

Li Zhi. *Zangshu.* Taibei: Taiwan Student Book Co., 1974.

Peng Wenqin, chief comp., and He Longxiang, ed. *Daozang jiyao.* Taibei: Xinwenfeng Publishing Co., 1977.

Sengyou. *Hongmingji.* Taibei: Xinwenfeng Publishing Co., 1974.

Yan Yiping, ed. *Daojiao yanjiu ciliao.* Taibei: Xiwen Printing Co., 1974.

Yeung Him-che. *Handbook of Chinese Herbs and Formulas.* Los Angeles: Institute of Chinese Medicine, 1985.

Yushu Zhenren. *Xianshu biku.* Taibei: Xinwenfeng Publishing Co., 1979.